4-23-63

87 MILLION JOBS

A Dynamic Program to End Unemployment

"Our population will increase from 180 to 208 million—up 28 million, or 15%—over the decade.

"The number of workers will grow faster, by nearly 20%—up 13.5 million to 87 million in 1970."— *Manpower, Challenge of the 1960's,* U.S. Department of Labor, 1960.

87 MILLION JOBS

*A Dynamic Program to
End Unemployment*

by THOMAS B. CURTIS

DUELL, SLOAN AND PEARCE
New York

First edition

Affiliate of
MEREDITH PRESS
Des Moines & New York

Library of Congress Catalog Number: 62-19794

MANUFACTURED IN THE UNITED STATES OF AMERICA
FOR MEREDITH PRESS

VAN REES PRESS • NEW YORK

ACKNOWLEDGMENTS

I would like to take this opportunity to thank those whose efforts have contributed to the preparation of this book. First I want to express my appreciation to the Congressmen, professors, Democrat, Republican, and independent; and other experts who participated in the House Republican Policy Committee's "Operation Employment," from which much of the factual information and many of the ideas of this work were formed. These include: Congressmen Edward Derwinski, William Scranton, John Rhodes, Clark MacGregor, Perkins Bass, John Anderson, Bruce Alger, Charles Mathias, William Springer, Charles Mosher, John Lindsay, Ben Reifel, Ross Adair, Ab Sibal, Silvio Conte, James Bromwell, William Cahill, Herman Schneebeli, Charles Goodell, Robert Dole, Melvin Laird, Robert Ellsworth, Catherine May, Walter McVey, Edwin Durno, William Ayres, Peter Garland, William Widnall, Paul Findley, Fred Schwengel, John Ashbrook, Jessica Weis, Bradford Morse, Ancher Nelsen, James Harvey, Don Short, Ralph Beermann, Robert Stafford, Clifford McIntire, James Battin, Glenard Lipscomb, and William Milliken;

Professors Goetz Briefs, Almarin Phillips, Clarence Long, Karl Brandt, Raymond Rodgers, Gottfried Haberler, Henry Wallich, William Fellner, Musa Hussayni, Yale Brozen, Michael Wermel, Father Joseph Becker, Robert Triffin, Wilson Schmidt, Colin Clark, Howard Ellis, Don Paarlberg, Bruno Hartung, Neil Jacoby, and Austin Murphy; and the Honorable True Morse, Louis Kelso, and Richardson Wood. I also appreciate the support of the Republican Policy Committee in the House of Representatives, its Chairman, Congressmen John Byrnes, and the Chairman of its Special Projects Subcommittee, Congressman John Rhodes. I want to acknowledge the assistance also of Dr. David Abshire and of Dr. Donald Ackerman, who contributed a study paper.

Particular thanks are due to Donald Webster, of the Joint Economic staff, and to Frederick Sontag, William Horton, Mrs. Marilyn Ballenger, Mrs. Thelma Shirley, and Mrs. Nell Siko, of my own office, all of whom assisted in the final preparation of the manuscript.

Two colleagues in the House deserve special thanks: Congressman Elmer J. Holland, for the fine work of his Subcommittee on Unemployment and the Impact of Automation, and Congressman Charles E. Goodell, for his leadership in drafting the final version of the Manpower Retraining Act and incorporating therein several of the recommendations made in this book.

I want to thank Professor Virgil Salera both for his participation in the Operation Employment study and for his research assistance in the preparation of the book and Karl Hess for editorial assistance in bringing it to its final form.

PREFACE

by ARTHUR F. BURNS

I first met Mr. Curtis when I served as Chairman of the Council of Economic Advisers. He was then, as he is now, a very active member of the Joint Economic Committee of the Congress. We did not always agree on economic issues. That is still the case. But I quickly learned to respect Congressman Curtis as a capable legislator, as a serious student of economic problems, and as a Republican leader who unfailingly pursued what he judged to be the nation's best interests.

Congressman Curtis' book reflects a conscientious search, which he has conducted over many years, for a solution to the recurring problem of unemployment. He laments and warns against reliance on governmental spending, which is nowadays commonly advanced as a cure for unemployment. The current problem, as he sees it, is not that jobs are unavailable for many workers, but rather that many workers are unsuited for the jobs that our advancing technology keeps creating.

This lively book is likely to stimulate fresh debates between those who regard a deficiency of aggregate spending and those who regard structural changes in the economy as the main cause of recent unemployment. As I see the facts, spending in one major branch of our economy—that is, on products of the capital goods industries—has recently been deficient, and this has served as a drag on aggregate demand. At the same time, I have no doubt that, in stressing the structural phases of unemployment, Mr. Curtis has captured an important part of the truth.

I have long felt that statistics on job vacancies are a vital missing link in our entire system of economic intelligence. Such statistics should be presented regularly on an over-all national basis, and they should also be classified along geographic, industrial, and occupational lines. Congressman Curtis has dramatized this need. I hope that those who dissent from his challenging views, no less than those who are inclined to accept them, will join him in urging the prompt establishment of the statistical system that we need to cope more intelligently with the problem of expanding employment opportunities.

PREFACE

by JOHN S. DICKEY
President, Dartmouth College

Congressman Curtis is probably more "from Missouri" than any many I have known. He personifies American pragmatism in his commitment to the integrity of a reality he can test. He is far from being a skeptic in his approach to life, but witnesses before the Ways and Means Committee or the Joint Economic Committee and, indeed, his closest friends have long known that to propound views at variance with reality, as Tom Curtis has observed it, is to be put politely but firmly to the proof of the variant proposition. And his questions are usually about as academic as the quills of an aroused porcupine—and frequently as difficult to be rid of.

The author of this little book is an academic only in his devotion to education and in his determination to study and understand anything to which he puts his hand. The reader will meet a man who believes both in the conservation of experience and that the answers to fundamental problems can only be created, not borrowed or bought.

PREFACE

by W. ALLEN WALLIS

Dean, Graduate School of Business
University of Chicago
President-elect, University of Rochester

The unemployment problem is one on which the facts are usually poorly understood and commonly misunderstood. The appropriateness of various solutions depends very much on what the facts are; solutions urged under one impression of the facts are seen, in the fuller light thrown on the facts by Mr. Curtis, to be useless or even harmful. He does not stop with discrediting the unsound solutions that occupy most of the stage in Washington, but proceeds to outline a sound program of governmental and private action.

Congressman Curtis is one of the most respected, influential, industrious, informed, and effective members of either house. Indeed, in the field of economics, no member of either house or either party is more respected than he, and very few indeed are his equals. He serves on both of the most important committees dealing with economic policy, the Committee on Ways and Means, in which all tax legislation originates, and the Joint Economic Committee, a committee including members of both houses which reviews domestic economic conditions and policies. He is a conservative, not in the sense of seeking to preserve the status quo or protect vested interests but—quite the contrary—in the sense that he seeks to conserve the forces of progress.

Even though I do not agree fully with everything that Mr. Curtis says in this book, I can recommend all of it as worthwhile and important. And when I have a chance to sit down with Tom Curtis and discuss the points on which we differ in view or emphasis, I know from previous experience that our differences will be considerably narrowed, partly by his persuasiveness and soundness but partly by his remarkable open-mindedness and intellectual honesty.

CONTENTS

87 MILLION JOBS

A Dynamic Program to End Unemployment

1. A CAPITAL CRIME

MILLIONS of jobs are going begging in America today, even while we are plagued by high unemployment. Our newspapers, if we read them closely, hammer this point home every day. On page one there is likely to be a story about high levels of unemployment. On the classified ad pages there will be column after column of job *openings*. The truth should be apparent. There are as many jobs available as there are persons without jobs. The problem is upgrading skills so that the unemployed *can* fill the jobs.

Oversimplified? Not really. Even when fleshed out with details, the challenge and the apparent answers remain the same. There are jobs. New skills are needed to fill them. Our future depends on it.

Unemployment is a capital crime which the citizens of an industrial nation commit against themselves. And it can be fatal.

Government policies and government programs can't really solve it. They can shuffle its statistics, sweep them

1

under the rug, give brief illusions of solution—and buy millions of votes in the process. But there is only one doorstep on which properly to place the guilt for failure really to eradicate this criminal waste of time, talent, and energy. Yours, ours.

It is our common misunderstanding of the matter, our common eagerness to seek solutions in public works rather than private initiative, that gives us the problem in the first place.

Here is how basic the proof of that is today:

There are about as many jobs going begging as there are persons officially classified as unemployed in this country.

The want ad section of any daily newspaper provides a clue to this. While government statistics drum away at the crisis of unemployment, the want ads drum away at the need, throughout industry and business, for able men and women to fill good and rewarding jobs.

Trade union pronouncements reflect the same paradox. There is immense concern about the "problem" of automation. There is minimum concern with ways in which to use to maximum this latest advance of machine technology—an advance which adds new strength and vigor to what could be the most exciting advance of the continuing industrial revolution. Today the exploitation of human muscle is no longer the key to material advances. It is the machine that is there to be exploited. From its wise use men, no longer encumbered by enslavement to the soil and weather, or to grinding tedium in the shop, can derive all the material substance they need and want.

Why aren't they doing so in full measure? Why is there still talk of unemployment when there are jobs aplenty? The answer is rather embarrassing. Many of us haven't taken the time to get as smart as the machines. People are lagging behind their mechanical creations. Men who have dreamed of an enlightened age in which the power of the mind would replace the ache of the back haven't been willing to take the steps that would really make the dream come true.

We are now persistently resisting the facts of the case in order to make drudgery and unskilled labor economically feasible as a way of life. We ignore the new jobs that a new age has created, and we concentrate, angrily, wistfully, confusedly, on the jobs at the lower end of the hiring scale that are being eliminated.

The attitude has become a national disgrace.

We can see its eroding effects everywhere. Our farm "problem" is a reflection of it. The total impact of the billions we spend each year to support farm prices is to keep marginal farm producers in business—as though there is something noble about virtually chaining a family to a slim subsistence farm, by a slim subsistence subsidy, rather than in making farming subject to the laws of supply and demand which govern our other industries and which, if left alone, would see literally millions of marginal farmers shake themselves loose from their bare-bone, hard-digging plots and start to move into industrial areas where, with no harder work, but with new training, they and their families could really begin to share the benefits of the twentieth century rather than just its charity.

The same is roughly true throughout industry. Any plan that attempts to "solve" the unemployment problem by perpetuating large blocs of jobs that have been outmoded merely aggravates the problem and avoids not just a solution but even an understanding of what the "problem" is in the first place.

The problem simply isn't unemployment. The problem is, as suggested at the outset, that there is a dislocation between the plenitude of jobs that are available and the skills needed to fill them.

The government approach, classically, has been to create jobs to fit available skills.

The really constructive approach, which is the responsibility of individuals, is to create skills to fill the jobs.

The truly challenging aspect of the situation is that no matter who you are, part of the solution lies in your hands.

If you work for wages and are unemployed, the solution may lie in mobility (going where the jobs are, rather than staying where they aren't) or training (reskilling to get one of the jobs that are available rather than waiting for some future opening in a dwindling field).

If you hold a union office or are active even as a voting member, part of the solution may lie in pressing for union actions and attitudes that strive to take advantage of machine technology advances, rather than in simply freezing workers and plants in the status-quo ice of outmoded machinery and outmoded jobs.

If you work with the tools of management, part of the solution may lie in shifting from defensive, play-it-safe attitudes to aggressive, competition-oriented, risk-taking actions that will expand horizons, not simply hold the line.

And for each of us, as voters, there is a vital portion of the solution in opposing policies which seek patent-medicine, short-term cures for employment dislocation rather than encouraging sound, long-range initiatives that will let people grow into new jobs.

The rule of thumb is obvious. Work *is* available. There *are* jobs that need to be filled. We don't need an increase in openings. We need an increase in the skills of our people so that they can do the work at hand. Any action that reverses this rule, seeking to create jobs artificially at skill-levels that are not actually needed, also reverses our chances for a full realization of this nation's future.

What is more, by filling jobs that now need to be filled we actually would create new jobs. Success begets success. Each filled job provides economic fuel for other jobs, as a pebble dropped in a pond produces expanding circles. By doing better in taking advantage of existing unfilled job opportunities, we expand the total number of opportunities as well.

In choosing our path, either backward to an economy of public work drudgery or forward to an economy of private initiative accomplishment, we cannot expect the rest of the world to be patient with mistakes we may make or to halt its own progress while we fumble and falter.

Today, in such a nation as West Germany, there is not only virtually no unemployment but there is such a demand for willing hands and minds that large-scale worker recruiting programs are being undertaken in neighboring nations.

Even in the so-called emerging nations there is an awakening realization that the solution to employment problems is the upgrading of skills—not the creation of jobs that the simplest tribesman can do in order to qualify for a government dole. If a nation like Nigeria understands this, and puts major efforts into upgrading its work skills, rather than in featherbedding outmoded skills, it should be possible for the most sophisticated free society on earth—ours—to do as much.

And yet, obviously, there is a massive inhibition against facing the simple facts of economic life when it comes to jobs in this country.

Rather than digging into the problem with the will and energy that opened up this nation in the first place, we still tend to reach for the soothing syrup of emergency relief programs, extended unemployment benefits, work-practice freezes, split-the-jobs hour shortening and other demonstrably useless or, at best, short-lived remedies. Why?

The answer seems to lie in a sort of national fear complex that is a hangover from the days of the prewar depression. The make-work economic thinking that won votes in those tragic days still has a magic ability to win votes in this day and age. So long as it does, the job of every American working man and manager, the investment of every saver, the profits of every enterprise, the chance of every dream for improvement, will be in grave and real peril.

So long as we behave and think in terms of the thirties we will directly risk a return to the depressions of the thirties.

It does no good to call an Administration of the latter half of the twentieth century the New Frontier if its economic thinking is traveling the tired old back-country road of the thirties.

Ever since the Second World War, in sharp contrast to the thirties, the key to prosperity in this country has been the *way* we work rather than simply the weight of our work. This dynamic economy has veered sharply from the past by creating new jobs, not simply more of the same kinds of old jobs. It has been creating skilled job needs which usually are not entirely filled—while, at the same time, it has been eliminating jobs at the lower end of the ladder of skills.

Today, as an example, electronic technicians are required by the tens of thousands. Mathematicians are the most sought-after "workers." For every pick-and-shovel job there are a score of openings for operators of earth-moving machines.

The only reason a cotton picker can find a job at all is because he will accept low wages. The only reason the operator of a cotton-picking *machine* can't find a job may be that he won't go where the job is waiting— at good wages.

Unfortunately, public emphasis has been placed almost entirely on the jobs that have been eliminated. The perfectly understandable cries of despair when an old factory closes down have been drowning out the busy sounds of work where a modern one has opened.

The sadder side of the picture cannot, of course, be ignored. Plant shutdowns involve individual human shocks and sometimes tragic ones. Wars do the same thing. But victories would never be won if the casualty lists entirely displaced battle planning in our thinking. The same thing applies to jobs.

Those who stand paralyzed by the blow of a shutdown, willing to do no more than wish for some benevolence from Washington to bring back the good old days, will never be able to contribute meaningfully to a realization of the even better new days.

As a nation we have paid the price of such shutdowns time and time again. But, as a rule, we have reaped the dividend of the job-creating new industries that are created concurrently.

From the shuttered, closed livery stables of the turn of the century, literally millions of new jobs have grown and flourished in the automobile industry.

From the painful piece work of the hand printer, the literacy-spurring giant presses have roared to life. There are probably living today men who saw their own world apparently come to an end with the collapse of the stereopticon slide business and the no-work signs on the doors of shops that made crystals and "cat whiskers" for early radios. Some may have well grown affluent, along with hundreds of thousands of others, in the new jobs created by modern radio and television.

There are reasons, of course, why the phenomenon of increased jobs—and better jobs—is not more widely recognized.

Most of the jobs develop as part of an initially quiet expansion of existing production operations or as virtually experimental efforts in some new field. (What did *you* think when you first heard that someone had left the security of a job in, say, the automobile industry to take a chance on some harebrained flyer such as building "space ships"?)

Even when such developments are recognized they are usually taken for granted. The collateral occurrence of a shutdown in some technology-bypassed area is never, however, taken for granted as a price of general growth.

Also, new jobs often develop far from where the old ones have come to an end. The automation of a plant in Los Angeles, causing local layoffs, may be outweighed by the stimulation of new and even better-paying jobs in St. Louis or Boston. But somehow the facts never seem to be put together. Bad news, unfortunately, makes more headlines than good.

Perhaps most important, however, is the fact that there is nothing in this dynamic system that automatically provides the man who has lost a job with one of the new and better jobs that has been created at the same time.

There are, however, barriers that may be built to make it less likely that the job and the man will get together as soon as possible. The biggest barrier can be set up by government, by consoling the jobless with federal spending programs, in return for which the worker has only to pay back with his vote come next election.

It would not be partisan or impolite to describe this as pure and simple bribery. Both parties have practiced it over the years. It is a sort of American tradition, at least since the thirties. The Administration in power

takes tax monies paid by all workers and sets up programs to provide a few workers with artificially created
jobs rather than encouraging the upgrading of skills that
would enable them to take on new and probably better
jobs with a real future.

The same sort of economic confidence game takes
place—again under both parties—in relation to the
industries that create the jobs in the first place.

Guiding the economic thinking of the nation for the
past generation has been the notion that all that needs
to be done to prime prosperity's pump is to increase
the consumption of goods and services. Witness the
common argument that extended unemployment benefits really provide an economic shot in the arm to industry because they provide extra consumer dollars.

Actually this is like saying that the only thing needed
to bring water out of the ground is a thirst.

The thing that really makes the wheels of a free
economy spin is the accumulation and availability of
savings—capital—with which to build the machines
and businesses that can *produce* the goods and services.
Then, and only then, can increased consumer spending
power have any meaning, because then and only then
will there be an expanding economic base to keep the
cycle of earning, saving, and spending going.

Only from such capital investments do we get new
jobs, new, solid consumer demand. Today it takes more
than twenty thousand dollars of saver-supplied capital,

on the average, to create a new job. The figure will be twenty-five thousand dollars before very long because of the increasing complexity of industrial technologies.

Our economy has never failed, so far, to come up with this vital capital investment. It will not fail to do so in the future, unless it is hamstrung by ill-conceived government policies. One of the most ill-conceived is the policy that attempts to make new jobs by draining off private savings to pay, by taxes, for massive government make-work programs. Such policies end in inflation; not in real employment, and never in real prosperity.

Even given the capital base, however, another element is crucial if we are realistically to face and understand our employment challenge. That element is the upgrading of skills.

There is nothing new about the concept. We've been doing it all along. What is new is the vital need to recognize and emphasize it.

Through company-sponsored training programs, or special educational efforts made by the individual himself, many a worker upgrades his skill to a level where his productivity is well above that of his former job.

When his old job becomes vacant, an individual below him on the skill ladder upgrades himself so that he can move into the spot. The same process of upgrading tends to occur across the whole of the industrial and service landscape, including men at most of the lowest rungs of the skill ladder. This, in general, is the nature of the process by which adjustments are made, involving literally millions of jobs each year. This is true job escalation.

After each individual has made the best job adjustment of which he is capable, an interesting thing happens to the national distribution of skills. Job escalation results in fewer persons working at the bottom of the skill ladder and more at every position above that level. Since the sum total of jobs keeps on increasing to satisfy the ever-growing desires of consumers, this means that the nation's work force enjoys more *and better* jobs. This, in essence, is what we mean by economic progress. It is also what the economists call the upward trend in real wages which has long been enjoyed by the American worker.

The beneficial effects are not confined to the individuals who move up the job ladder. There are at least four broader effects. One consists of greater income equality, which is achieved as the lowest-paying jobs slowly decline in relative importance. This highly desirable result is attained, moreover, without—by taxation—robbing Peter to pay Paul.

Contrast this process with the sledge-hammer spending of government make-work schemes. Such schemes have pounded us into what is now a colossal misfit of skills in our economy. A hard reality is that the spending emphasis has also sidetracked our pricing system's role in developing a good skill-structure of jobs. We've overlooked fundamentals. How many times have we overpriced unskilled labor, only to gloss over it by resorting to massive doses of spending medicine? Unemployment has been made worse by the *under*pricing of skilled and technical talent and the overpricing of jobs at the bottom of the skill ladder.

Another effect is that economic growth is accelerated, as each member of the work force makes contributions geared closer to his maximum potential. Moreover, an upward trend in real wage income produced by job escalation increases each individual's ability to provide directly for his own family's welfare needs and thus gives promise of tax relief, for which most Americans yearn. Finally, job escalation provides a sound means for increasing personal incomes while simultaneously helping to improve America's competitive international economic position.

This analysis does not mean that government has no role to play regarding the ways and means of producing high-level employment. But federal government spending, of the kind which has been advocated during most of the last few decades, will not come to grips with the tasks that have to be performed if job skills are to be kept in line with changing job requirements across the land. The philosophy of spending merely threatens us with an artificially stimulated demand for products and services already embodying the scarcest skills. Hence, the position of those having relatively unwanted skills is worsened, not improved. For the economy as a whole the result, as has been stated, is inflation, or controls over the economy that only suppress inflation—and, in the process, suppress liberties as well.

Actually government has much to contribute to a positive program of lifting the level and quality of American employment. Such contributions would not be concerned with the usual so-called "stabilization" spending measures. Rather, government's contributions should be directed toward the multidimensional requirements of upgrading skills, expanding labor mobility, and increasing the inducements to save and invest so that America may have more capital, better management, and a more skilled work force.

Against this background, we now move to specifics and details.

2. THE PATH TO MORE GOVERNMENT

IF JOBS, their changing, creation, and loss, are one of our most natural preoccupations now, so are they also the subject of the most divisive political debate our nation has ever undertaken.

Unemployment once was a simple matter for most Americans to discuss. Cal Coolidge, for example, said that when there is a scarcity of jobs, unemployment results. But that was also at a time when the concept of jobs was fairly simple. To make a job, someone had to make an investment—to meet a probable demand for goods or services. The grocery clerk saved his money to open a store of his own. The mechanic saved his money to open a small plant of his own. The rich shifted money to new enterprises that promised better markets. When Henry Bessemer conceived a better way to make steel, it was accumulated capital that turned the blueprint into furnaces—and into thousands, hundreds of thousands of new jobs, paying better wages to the workingmen whose skills could match the new processes' demands.

And the nation grew as savings built new plants and businesses, which required new skills and created new jobs. Then, and only then, were new markets and new demands created, which resulted in sales and profits from which new savings could be accumulated to keep the process moving forward. Somewhere along the line, however, a significant number of academic observers of the process decided it needed drastic overhauling. Among the reasons advanced for the need were these:

The old system tended to channel wealth toward the most energetic members of the society and not necessarily toward the most needful members.

The system emphasized productivity and left the provision of cultural services up to individual initiative. Where the academicians could clearly recognize that everyone needed enlarged exposure to music and art, the sponsorship of such things as art galleries and symphonies still depended upon the rich and energetic who might, almost as though by whim, someday decide to build another factory rather than another band shell. Thus, the accumulated wealth had to be removed from such potentially selfish control and placed at the disposal of the community and the needs which the academicians evaluated as proper for the community.

Very importantly, in terms of jobs, the old system meant periods of dislocation as the supply and demand for skills was affected by new processes and markets. Take the emphasis off capital and place it on consumption, reasoned the theorists of a new system, and planning could be more orderly—because the government, by controlling money flow, could also control consumption.

The basis for employment, then, becomes simply the creation of more consumer spending. This is, of course, precisely the crisis in economic thought mentioned in the preceding chapter, repeated here to carry it the one step farther needed to make it fit exactly into consideration of concrete actions to get on with the work of substituting jobs for jawing in the current discussion of employment and unemployment. The step is simply that of making government the prime factor in job creation rather than continuing enterprise and investment as the prime factor.

Today, as a matter of demonstrable fact, it is just that sort of step, widely accepted as "right," that is digging us deeper into employment problems rather than letting our native energy build a better answer.

Perhaps the most influential academic economist in the country today is Professor Paul Samuelson of the Massachusetts Institute of Technology. His *Economics, An Introductory Analysis* has already gone to five editions in thirteen years, and reportedly has sold more than one million copies. Hundreds of universities require use of the book. It is a potent promulgator of one approach to employment.

What does Professor Samuelson say about the problem of employment in our dynamic economy? He summarizes his position in three pages of his book. It goes about like this:

New and improved ways of producing goods and services throw men out of work—unless production is increased.

Our consuming public could conceivably absorb a larger total output, but we can't, and dare not, count on such a result.

Instead, we must aim to have enough new jobs for our people, which is said to require little if anything more than an increase in new dollar purchasing power. This is the task of the federal government, using fiscal and monetary policies. That is, Washington could cut taxes while government spending is left unchanged, or it could increase government spending by incurring debt-raising government deficits, or it could make bank credit cheap and easy to get at the nation's commercial banks. Any one of these, or some combination of the three, will do the job of increasing the supply of purchasing power and, consequently, jobs.

An only slightly different view was expressed in response to a question which I put to Dr. Walter Heller, chairman of President Kennedy's Council of Economic Advisers, in hearings dealing with the President's Economic Report. My question concerned the impact of rapid technological progress on employment. In reply, the Joint Economic Committee of the Congress was told: "So long as overall demand for labor remains strong, the displaced workers will be absorbed into areas of expanding employment."

The foregoing, in a nutshell, is the new employment policy. It is, actually, depression economics. Because some men temporarily lose jobs in our dynamic economy, it is assumed that a *general* deficiency of purchasing power just naturally and automatically results. There is no room in the assumption for awareness that it is the same dynamic economy's *creation of new jobs* which results in some old jobs being displaced.

Moreover, the spending approach doesn't view the purchasing power aspects in an even passably realistic way. Consider, for instance, how typical business investment in new technology is related in time to increased total production in the economy. The important fact is that such investment involves expenditures —which become a part of the community's spendable income—*before* new output comes on the market. In simple purchasing power terms, we get a net increase in spending power before we get an expansion in the volume of production which competes for the consumers' dollars.

Such a development, in and of itself, increases employment even according to or despite the new prescriptions. And this is what usually happens, in fact, when the economy is permitted by Washington to proceed in its own dynamic way. The increased employment, however, does not show up uniformly over the whole range of job skills. In other words, many individuals with low-order skills do not find jobs, despite Dr. Heller's assertion that they are "absorbed into areas of expanding employment."

It is this point which is tragically slighted in the government approach. Jobs are looked upon as a simple pliable mass locked up in a squeezable plastic dispenser, with government-dictated spending policies constituting the pressure which squeezes out just enough jobs to go around. (The polyethelene dispenser, incidentally, is a convenient product which some economists now love to classify as a mere "gadget." Yet it is one of the millions of new and useful commodities turned out by our dynamic economy and on which new jobs are created. About 30 per cent of our new products were not on the market as recently as five years ago.)

Regarding the question of employment, however, one misses the key problem by viewing jobs as things which government spenders can squeeze out at will. The truth is that government spending only unbalances the job pattern to the disadvantage of those whose skill is of a low order or obsolete.

In fairness to the spenders, though, it may be admitted that a few persons who should be upgraded are

likely to find work for a time in their old skill as a part
of the economic distortions which sheer inflation produces. But the vast majority of those in need of upgrading unfortunately will remain unemployed. People so
affected by government policy are also a drag on the
economy's growth. The persistence of such employment
is the tragedy of a naked spending policy.

In summary, the public spending approach errs
fundamentally in regarding the employment problem as
one that melts away as soon as government controls
produce the "right volume" of spending. Today, it is
necessary to face up to the need for direct action in the
area of job escalation, not the hit-or-miss methods of
the spenders. Our primary task is that of upgrading individuals to match the unfilled jobs generated by our
dynamic economy. We need to recognize this because
so much of our unemployment is as impervious to the
cutting edge of spending *per se* as water is to scissors.

Two factors should constantly be borne in mind in
formulating policy:

First, consumers know best how to take care of their
own spending and don't need to be told when and how
much to spend.

Second, government spending policies in themselves
do not even help to meet America's key employment
problem, which is that of matching up most individual
workers with the right jobs—better jobs—in an ever-
changing job market.

If the economy is to achieve the growth rate of which it is capable—which is well above that recorded in recent times—it will have to be permitted to operate realistically. In particular, improving the nation's job structure is a challenge which must be faced directly by people in the community, private industry, organized labor, and in addition, some agencies of the federal government.

Before we plunge into action, it is necessary that we recognize what this challenge really is. We need to appreciate the nature of the many-wheeled mills of job adjustment in a dynamic economy.

There is the need for special kinds of information not now available in the community.

The integrity of the country's unemployment compensation system must be preserved.

The schools have a vital role to play, in relation to local as well as more distant job markets.

Our tax laws need to be changed so as to assist rather than hinder job adjustment.

Deterrents to business efforts in job retraining must be swept away.

Inducements to business investment must be geared to the problems associated with upgrading of the nation's manpower, and this must be done in a new and far-sighted manner.

In fact, nearly everything but the old-fashioned federal spending formula needs to be used!

Contrast this line-up of needs with the simple response which Dr. Heller, President Kennedy's economic adviser, made to my query about the impact of rapid technological progress on employment. He stressed more federal spending, adding as an afterthought that work in the field of retraining would also help. Clearly, he has his priorities thoroughly confused. We only add insult to the injury of those who are the chief victims of unemployment when we pretend that the shotgun methods of deficit finance are the answer to the employment problem in a dynamic economy.

We need, instead, exactly the sort of weapon that served our forefathers on their frontier—a rifle of great accuracy with which to hit a target of great urgency.

3. THE INFLATION FACTOR

IT IS important that we achieve maximum employment, with jobs for all who are able and willing to work. But it is equally important to prevent inflation. Rising prices rob our people, and particularly those in the lower income groups, of the compensation they receive for their labor. If the pay check buys less each year, the attainment of maximum employment becomes a hollow achievement. In effect, when you need more and more money units to buy just the same amount of goods and services, or even less, you are taking a cut in pay. Your job is weakened. Your economy is weakened. Just having more people at work becomes an illusion under such a circumstance. It is simply a way of spreading poverty; not building prosperity.

To face our employment challenge realistically we must also face this factor of inflation, understand it, and do something about it (In subsequent chapters three other key factors will be discussed: the persistence of unemployment in some areas, the centralization and growing cost of government, and an unnecessarily weak international economic posture.)

Ever since the Employment Act of 1946, we have been trying to maintain employment by relying mainly on the spending of government.

The result of such policy, in terms of our official price statistics, has been more or less chronic inflation rather than the correct level and pattern of employment. The erosion of the dollar's purchasing power has been at the rate of about 2 per cent to 3 per cent a year for some periods, though there have also been short intervals of relatively stable prices.

The war left a legacy of pent-up demands and piled-up liquidity. That is, the shift to war output rendered unavailable a long list of goods, especially those of the durable variety, and, in addition, accumulated holdings of government securities represented available purchasing power for use—on top of current incomes—as soon as civilian goods once more were stocked by the nation's shops.

The government, after the war, continued to stand ready to buy government securities at fixed prices—a policy called "monetizing the debt." This policy of "bond pegging" finally succumbed to persistent attack, largely directed by Senator Paul Douglas in now-celebrated hearings before the Joint Economic Committee of the Congress.

Our bad experience with bond pegging after the war

is important enough to merit some retelling. There is
no better way than to cite some testimony which Mr.
William McChesney Martin, the distinguished and cour-
ageous Chairman of the Federal Reserve Board, presented before the Joint Economic Committee in
connection with hearings on the 1961 Economic Report of the President. Mr. Martin started off by relating
the mechanics of bond pegging: the Federal Reserve
Banks provided the government with funds required
but not raised through taxation—

> "by buying outstanding government securities on a
> huge scale. The Federal Reserve's payments for
> these securities wound up in bank reserves. In turn,
> the banking system used these additional reserves
> to purchase new securities that the Treasury was
> issuing to obtain further funds to finance the war
> effort.
>
> "To keep the process going, the Federal Reserve
> in effect maintained a standing offer to buy govern-
> ment securities in unlimited amount at relatively
> fixed prices, set high enough to assure that their
> interest rates or yields would be pegged at pre-
> determined low levels. When no one else would
> accept those yields and pay those prices, the Fed-
> eral Reserve did so. And in so doing, it helped to
> finance the war.
>
> "The process was certainly successful for its
> emergency purpose. But the procedure of pegging
> government securities at high prices and low yields

entailed a price of its own that the economy—the people and the government alike—would later have to pay. The results were twofold:

"1. During wartime, money was created rapidly and continually, in effect setting a time bomb for an ultimate inflationary explosion—even though the immediate inflationary consequences were held more or less in check by a system of direct controls over prices, wages, materials, manpower, and consumer goods.

"2. The market for government securities became artificial. The price risks normally borne by participants in that market were eliminated: bonds not payable for twenty years or more became the equivalent of interest-bearing cash since they could be turned into cash immediately at par value or better—at the option of the owners, at any time."

Once committed to spending programs, government officials, from the President on down, must risk creating "time bombs for ultimate inflationary explosions." They must keep on spending and, in the process, must concoct all manner of arguments to distract attention from the simple fact that the kettle of inflation continues on the boil. As Mr. Martin put the matter, bond pegging "entailed a price of its own that the economy would later have to pay." The postwar inflation is a silent witness to the consequences.

The pent-up demand and the piled-up liquidity resulting from the war, however, was not to last indefinitely. In fact, they were probably not major inflationary factors for as much as half of the postwar period.

What considerations, then, account for the country's more or less continued creeping inflation? Students of the problem list several causes: a huge government budget, a large welfare establishment, and, especially, a combination of substantial increases in the quantity of money in conjunction with the "wage-push" of strong labor unions.

Some observers add what they term "administered-price" inflation, or price increases allegedly dictated by strategically placed sellers. Following Harvard's Professor Gottfried Haberler, however, I find that there is no reason to assume that markups in the business area are continuously increased. Some people have made such an assumption essentially as a deduction from the theoretical proposition that in some industries prices may be at a higher level than would prevail under conditions of simple textbook competition.

A word is immediately in order respecting the differences between the economic position of strong business sellers and strong, rigidly disciplined labor unions. As Professor Haberler has shown in his *Inflation, Its Causes and Cures* (Washington, D. C.: American Enterprise Association, 1961), there are three basic differences:

First, unions are able to hold wage rates rigid on the down-side and biased on the up-side. Most business sellers, in sharp contrast, are forced to sell at lower prices nearly every time the economy's pace slackens a little, and profits suffer in consequence.

Second, businessmen have a weaker bargaining position than strong unions. This is because business sellers lack basic strengths enjoyed by unions: physical coercive power, rigid discipline, and/or intense member loyalty.

Third, unions are exempt from the antimonopoly laws while businesses are not.

It is natural that unions wish to improve the position of their members. This aim is also rightly established in the laws of the land. What is questionable, however, is action forcing large wage increases yearly or every other year—increases so large that they must result in price rises which hurt everyone.

The worst cases are those which unfortunately are supported by the widely held belief that productivity increases in any *one* industry are a proper yardstick for wage-fixing in that industry. Such a yardstick is faulty. Productivity grows unevenly among industries. The national average has been about 2 per cent, but in some of the most dynamic industries productivity obviously expands at a higher rate than the average while in others the rate of increase is under 2 per cent.

Given this unevenness, wages based on each industry's productivity situation would soon produce very wide wage differentials.

A policy of tying wages to each industry's productivity would prevent price reductions, since the industries which would otherwise experience falling costs find instead that the union has driven a wage bargain that prevents cost reduction. The rest of us as consumers would also like to receive some of the benefits of falling costs in the form of lower prices. Historically, such price reductions have helped to offset price increases in industries not blessed with favorable technological or resource conditions, so that we enjoyed in the past a kind of built-in moderator of inflationary forces stemming from loose government spending.

Briefly, then, above-average productivity increases in a particular industry do not justify above-average wage advances. The facts, incidentally, are that wages have been forced up at some 3 per cent to 3½ per cent a year on the average, while productivity has been rising about 2 per cent, so that prices have been rising one to 1½ times due to this cause alone.

Contrast to this the effects of a vigorous program of upgrading the labor force. We could then enjoy rising real wages due less to union pressure and more to superior performance, keep costs from rising as they have been, and thus enjoy more stable prices. The individual worker would be better off, and the community would benefit from stable prices. Our economy would also gain on the international front, because United States prices would be more competitive in world markets.

What has been happening abroad is of an approximately parallel nature. Wage settlements in excess of productivity gains, for instance, are the very excesses which British observers list as being most responsible for the weakness in their economy. Thus, *The Economist* of London laments the "collective bludgeoning" by unions, under which workers exact more money "before they have earned it," with the result that there is an inflationary weakening of Britain's economic position. This distinguished journal also agreed with the conclusion of a panel of experts for the Organization for European Economic Cooperation (including Yale's Professor William Fellner) that Britain's inflation had been due chiefly to wage-push. Two other countries shared the same dubious distinction, Denmark and the United States. The OEEC added that it was "significant that economic growth was less vigorous in these three countries" than in any other nations studied. The OEEC might have added that two of the three, Britain and the United States, have also suffered in recent years from serious loss of international confidence in the strength of their currencies.

Such inflationary wage increases as have been described above can be brought to a halt—if the nation is prepared to pay the price. But this would require a sizable amount of unemployment, and nobody wants that. Let me illustrate in terms of the experience of 1959. A strong inflationary psychology and wage-push was in evidence at the time, fanned by a record peace-time budget deficit of $12.4 billion in fiscal year 1959. The kettle of inflation was menacingly on the boil, and the position of the dollar was weakening dangerously. It was felt necessary, in consequence, to administer strong medicine. A sharp budgetary change was made, from a record deficit in the previous fisical year to a small surplus in the budget beginning July 1, 1959. In addition, there was a sharp turnaround in monetary policy, as bank reserves were kept tight. The yield on Treasury bills, for example, rose from a low of 0.88 per cent in mid-1958 to a record 4.6 per cent in late 1959. Perhaps the medicine was somewhat too strong or ap-plied a little too long. Some such doubts are raised because the business upswing was a good deal shorter than the previous postwar expansions had been. In any event, despite the medicine, it is worth emphasizing that the next year saw the emergence of a real "gold scare" and for the first time in decades a genuine concern for the position of the dollar in world markets.

In the typical situation, however, no attempt is made to use medicines, and the money supply is allowed merrily to move upwards in order to accomodate the wage-push, and/or our fiscal policy calls for govern-ment deficits for achieving the same purpose.

What has such a policy done for employment?

We continue to experience substantial unemployment, which some writers even call "hard core" joblessness. We must clearly conclude, I submit, that inflation is no answer to the job problem, to say nothing of the social harm which results from its force.

There is no denying that we have suffered from inflation. At the same time, it is necessary to emphasize that the official statistics exaggerate the upward movement of prices. They do so in several ways. Most of all, they fail to take proper account of improvements in the *quality* of products and services, and they also are very slow in reflecting the many new products which become available to consumers. As a result, a given year's reported 2 per cent rise in prices, for example, really represents a rise of well under 2 per cent. Perhaps this point may be more meaningfully illustrated in terms of developments which occur in the automobile industry. We know definitely, for instance, that increases in the prices of automobiles during the 1950's were overstated as a result of the failure of the government statisticians to take account of horsepower, weight, length, and so forth.

Strangely enough, the official statistics' overstatement of price increases actually has worked to intensify realized inflation. This is one of the findings made by the Price Statistics Review Committee of the National Bureau of Economic Research, chaired by Professor George Stigler of the University of Chicago.

This Committee's report, made at the request of the Office of Statistical Standards of the Bureau of the Budget, was also the subject of hearings before the Joint Economic Committee of the Congress. I well recall these hearings and some of the sensational findings brought out by the professional witnesses. For example, consider the field of collective bargaining agreements. A number of these call for wage increases whenever the consumer price index rises by a certain percentage.

It is this same sort of preoccupation with quantities rather than with qualities that plagues every aspect of the employment situation.

The quality of products, as just described, must be reflected to make quantity of product and price statistics realistic.

The quality as well as quantity of dollars in our economy must be reflected to make the impact of inflation understandable.

The quality as well as quantity of jobs must be reflected in our considerations in order to avoid some future day in which a man may be elected President of this nation by wildly proclaiming that he will abolish machinery and "create" all the new jobs needed by returning us to a pick and shovel economy in building roads and homes and to hand production lines in building automobiles. That is precisely the promise which, ultimately, our current clinging to the past in our employment considerations give us.

The great pyramids and the Great Wall of China were both projects that provided jobs aplenty, not for a free market, but for the vanity of theories (theological and political rather than economic). They also provided the makers and monuments of dead civilizations. And so would such works in our time.

4. THEORIES FIRST, FACTS TO FIT

In discussing unemployment in America there is a detail that persistently makes the going rather rough. Our government, so far, has been unable to provide meaningful figures as to just how many Americans want work and can't find it. In such a statistical vacuum it has long been feasible to concoct a theory and then find the figures that conveniently fit it.

Today's most obvious fad of the sort is to chart a rising tide of unemployed persons, place it alongside production charts, income charts, and spending charts, and then conclude that if someone (usually the federal government) just would spend more money there would be more demands for production, more need for workers, and then, wondrous to behold, jobs for all.

Such exercises undoubtedly provide employment for a number of statisticians. They have never provided many jobs for anyone else.

The confusion stretches all the way from the figures

involved to the definitions of employment and unemployment themselves.

An interesting example which should have, but obviously did not, cause some serious new looks at the situation came to light in April, 1959, when the Swedish government experimented with the American method of collecting unemployment figures.

As a welfare state Sweden is, of course, quite sensitive to statistics of employment and unemployment. The employment statistics are the source of the staggering tax takes which finance extensive social welfare programs, including those for the unemployed. At the time, Sweden was under the impression that there were only 47,000 of its citizens who could properly be described as unemployed.

To check this, the American sampling method of checking unemployment (which will be discussed in detail) was tried.

The result was disconcerting, to say the least. By our definition and technique, it turned out that there weren't 47,000 Swedes out of work, but rather three times that many—136,000!

On paper, poor Sweden had suddenly been plunged into one of the most depressed eras in its history. As in America, there were undoubtedly many economists who immediately reached for new and more stringent government spending medicines to cure the raging fever. Fortunately, the patient was returned to health by simply tearing up the diagnosis.

Almost as basic as the statistical confusion about unemployment is the semantic one.

Economists talk about frictional, structural, and cyclical unemployment. There are as many meanings for each as there are theories for solving the problem.

Frictional unemployment reflects job obsolescence, itself the by-product of our dynamic economy. Popularly, however, it is believed that such an economy only produces job displacement, not obsolescence. Newspapers and magazine and broadcast commentators are particularly fond of giving this impression. Labor union leaders also often speak to the same point. But job displacement is less than half of the truth.

The dynamic American economy really does two things simultaneously: it creates new jobs and at the same time renders some old ones obsolete. The latter represents most of the frictional unemployment, which is of short duration. This category of unemployment would also include persons who voluntarily abandon jobs while searching for something for which they are also technically qualified but which may be more attractive or better paying.

Structural unemployment involves the permanent decline of a major industry or a permanent decline in job opportunities in such an industry. Coal is a good illustration. It has come to occupy a relatively smaller place in the structure of our economy, and it has also been subject to mechanization, which has rendered some skills permanently obsolete.

Those who believe that we can spend our way into full employment, amplify these definitions with a lexicon strictly their own. It goes something like this:

First, they observe accurately that technological progress make certain kinds of production possible with less labor per unit of output. Next, however, they define the "leftover" labor (which I would describe as having been rendered technologically obsolete) as having been "released." In simple mechanistic fashion, therefore, they say that it needs to be merely "reabsorbed." And how is it to be reabsorbed (i.e., put back at roughly the same work that the technological progress was supposed to displace)? By increased aggregate spending, by government monetary policy that will put more spendable cash into consumer hands even if only by more unemployment payments, and by direct federal spending if need be.

No sounder scheme could be devised for assuring the growth of unemployment and the persistence of its chief cause: the failure of skills to keep pace with the technological advances which, at one and the same time, render some jobs obsolete while creating a demand for people to fill newly created but more highly skilled ones.

Our country suffers from far more structural unemployment than is necessary. It does so largely because we have failed to cope with frictional unemployment. We have failed primarily because we have not done nearly enough to equip with new skills those whose old skills are rendered obsolete by rapid technological progress. Note: not just technological progress, but *rapid* progress. As I have emphasized in various committees of the Congress and on the floor of the House, structural unemployment which is of long duration, is essentially the result of frictional unemployment that has been left unsolved.

This is the most important single technical reason why the United States has to get on with a sensible system for upgrading the skills of her people. There is no reason why we cannot keep the pattern of skills and the distribution of individuals having appropriate skills abreast of technological advance.

The spend-our-way-out alternative has not worked, will not work, cannot work.

Perpetuating the confusion is the numbers game mentioned earlier.

A person is officially regarded as unemployed:

If he is fourteen years of age or older and is not at work and . . .

States that he is looking for a job, or . . .

Is waiting to be called back to the employment from which he had been laid off, or . . .

Is willing to report to a new job scheduled to start within thirty days (but he must not be in school), or . . .

Would have been looking for employment except that he was (a) temporarily ill or (b) *believed* that no job was available in his community in his line of work.

It is easy to see that this is no simple definition; more importantly, it is perhaps the most all-inclusive definition of unemployment to be found anywhere in the world.

From the technical point of view, perhaps the central feature of the official definition is that it is the person reached by a Census Bureau interview who decides for himself whether he is out of work and seeking employment. The Census Bureau does little if any checking as to whether a person who says he is looking for work is really doing so.

The whole operation rests on what the statisticians call a "sample" of the population. A midmonthly figure on unemployment is arrived at, but not by attempting to make a complete count one by one. That would be far too costly, and only very slightly better than the results which are obtained by a careful sample. Instead of attempting an exact count, then, interviews are arranged with 35,000 families in 333 areas across the nation, pretty much after the fashion of public opinion polls. Such a sampling provides a cross-section picture, so that a reasonably accurate report is obtained as far as the statistical procedures are concerned.

It is the questions asked and the system of classifying answers which have proved troublesome to the specialists in the subject. If the person interviewed is at work, he is obviously classified as employed. When, however, such a person is not employed, he will be listed as unemployed if he states that his case falls into one of the categories previously given. One of these has to do with whether the individual was "looking for work." What does this mean? We find that the Census Bureau takes the respondent's word for it. But this clearly means that all manner of situations can fall under the heading of "looking for a job."

Every respondent is treated as a "unit" in this method of gathering statistics. But herein lies a source of confusion to the public, which regards the official unemployment data, quite understandably, as indicators of the country's economic health.

Specifically, consider three types of individuals: the steelworkers out of work, the teen-ager who is still in school but would like a summer job even though he lacks a skill that is in demand (and doesn't want to commute a long distance to an unskilled job which may be available), and a man retired from his regular work on social security but still wanting a job that fits his particular circumstances.

Two features of this list deserve attention. First, given our modern and highly productive economy, in contrast to a peasant economy where everybody must pitch in if they are to survive, one of our public purposes is to create a society in which some people don't work. The retired man on social security is a case in point. He can and perhaps should afford to be very selective in considering employment. Yet if he is, and the Census Bureau interviews him only to find that he is still looking, he is counted as unemployed no less than the jobless steelworker with a family to support from wages. Second, some means should be found for segregating classes of unemployment so that our official figures distinguish between the real cases and the types that fall very close to the situations in which people purposefully are not at work. The Labor Department is now supposedly segregating teen-ager and retired unemployment; but this is only for special purposes. The Department continues to publish the Census Bureau's questionable total figure about which the general public hears so much.

The interpretation of any given official figure of unemployment must also take account of changes in the number of people included in what is called the "labor force."

Though every person at work last month may still be on the job during the current month, unemployment may have increased in the interval. The reason is that some people not previously at work have decided to enter the work force: a housewife, say, to supplement her husband's income, or teen-age students who would like to have temporary jobs.

Furthermore, surveys by the Census Bureau show

that, in a typical year, for every three persons officially listed as unemployed, there are about two individuals holding down not one but a pair of paying jobs— "moonlighting."

However, no allowance is made for moonlighting in figuring the unemployment total. A really effective system of upgrading the work force, such as the one I will describe later, should be able to replace two average jobs with one good one.

The United States usually shows a high rate of joblessness. This pleases the Communists, I might add, who everlastingly stress the point in their propaganda work throughout the world. Our relatively high rate is partly due to the all-inclusiveness of the United States concept of employment statistics. It also results in a sense from international differences in the way unemployment is measured. Only we and Canada use a sampling procedure of the kind outlined above. Most foreign countries formally register persons who are unemployed. During the process, each is asked relevant questions about his job-seeking. The result, as a rule, is that foreign countries treat unemployment statistically in a much more restricted fashion than we do.

Our loose definition of unemployment can be responsible for pushing the country into dubious remedies. For example, many officials in Washington would use an arbitrary percentage rate of unemployment as the criterion for automatically starting massive new federal spending programs. Massive federal spending—of your tax dollars and mine—tied to shaky statistics certainly will not do the job.

We have a state-administered unemployment insurance program in America. This program supplies an unquestionably more accurate measure of the amount of unemployment in the economy. It is high time, I suggest, that we made more use of it in public discussions of the problem, and particularly in our various analyses of economic policy.

5. TWO VIEWS OF ONE PROBLEM

DURING hearings on the President's Economic Report before the Joint Economic Committee, I asked President Kennedy's Council of Economic Advisers why it did not relate the high rate of unemployment which exists among the unskilled and semiskilled to the rapid technological growth which prevails in our society. The Council's reply made two points. The first was that this special impact of technology upon the indicated groups was not a new phenomenon. Secondly, and I think more importantly, Mr. Kennedy's economic advisers stated that "the pattern of labor supply can in time, and in a favorable economic environment [more spending?], adapt to the pattern of demand. If the demand for skilled and white-collar labor were more active, more transfer into these groups would occur."

A second question to the Council was directed more specifically to the job impact of our growing economy. I asked for comment on my view that unemployment, instead of being the result of a tired, sluggish, or

sick economy, as has been asserted, arises mainly because the economy has been *growing* so fast. In reply,
the Council of Economic Advisers neatly sidestepped
the issue by arguing that "It is impossible to accept current levels of unemployment as simply the growing
pains of a rapidly growing economy because there is no
independent evidence that the economy is growing
rapidly." The Council added that dynamic growth en-
tails some job redundancy, but felt that we need not be
concerned because "we have solved these problems in
the past." The past solutions, of course, included the
stimulation of spending to hold people in obsolete jobs.

But, just as important, what was meant by the charge
that there is an absence of *independent* evidence that
the economy is growing rapidly? Does that deny that
millions of jobs are going begging in the United States
because new skill requirements cannot be met owing to
skill obsolescence and too slow a rate of new skill
development?

These jobs are not going begging because American
industry is stagnated for want of greater aggregate
spending, as the untested Council theory would have it.
The unfilled job vacancies, for which, incidentally, we
still do not have good statistics, are the result of dynamic
growth—new industries, the vigorous application of
scientific progress by American industrial management,
and the keen and growing interest of our consumers in

new products and services of all kinds (some of them provided by state and local governments, such as is the case in the field of education).

In an important sense, the Council holds to a dangerous view that ours is an economy plagued by a chronic deficiency of demand, which can only be offset by massive deficit-financed federal spending schemes. How can we reconcile this view with the fact that our total national production has more than doubled in half a generation since the war? The Council's theory simply can't be squared with the relevant facts.

Given also the struggle between the free world and its totalitarian enemies, there is an even more alarming feature in the Council's position. It lacks faith in the capacity of our free private enterprise economy to generate high-level employment, as Professor Arthur F. Burns has stated in a public debate with President Kennedy's economic advisers. I thoroughly agree with Professor Burns, himself a distinguished former Chairman of the Council of Economic Advisers under President Eisenhower, when he implored Mr. Kennedy's Council not to "exaggerate the shortcomings of our economy or belittle the achievements of the past." Burns could have added that a program of belittlement only tends to depress private business. Is not most of the belittlement really aimed at a dead end, at expansion of the size and cost of government?

I also agree with Professor Burns's conviction that more Americans should understand that we can take pride in having achieved great gains under our enterprise system, itself the main pillar of our free society. I would like to repeat a profound observation of his: "Perhaps the greatest economic triumph of our generation, although we too often show little appreciation of it, is the reduction of the swings of the business cycle and the blunting of their impact on the lives and fortunes of individuals." These are not the words of an ordinary economist, for Professor Burns is one of the foremost living students of business fluctuations. If we can succeed in rapidly upgrading the skills of the American people, as I firmly believe we can once we give the spending panaceas a decent burial, we can add a new measure of progress to the firm stabilization base which Professor Burns has described.

The same hearings on the President's Economic Report also contain an interesting exchange of views on employment policy between the Federal Reserve Board and President Kennedy's Council of Economic Advisers. Highlights of the exchange between these two influential Washington institutions are revealing and vital to understanding of the employment picture.

The Federal Reserve Board is the independent agency of the government which is responsible for handling the nation's monetary and credit policy. This thankless but indispensable task inevitably impinges upon all of those —including the national government—who borrow funds. Thus, when the credit supply has to be tightened in the interest of a more stable economy and as partial insurance against serious inflation, the Federal Reserve does not win many popularity contests.

Appearing before the Joint Economic Committee of the Congress, Federal Reserve Chairman Martin shared his views regarding the seriousness of the unemployment problem, and then pointed to the contracyclical operations which the Federal Reserve was conducting especially in an effort to combat that part of unemployment caused by a general economic slide-off. Since he was really concerned most of all with structural unemployment, his comments were directed chiefly to this matter. Mr. Martin's statement seems to me to be so eminently wise that I wish to cite it at some length:

> To have important effect, attempts to reduce structural unemployment by massive monetary and fiscal stimulation of overall demands probably would have to be carried to such lengths as to create serious new problems of inflationary character—at a time when consumer prices already are at a record high.
>
> Actions effective against structural unemployment and free of harmful effects therefore need to be specific actions that take into account the who,

the where, and the why of unemployment, and, accordingly, go to the core of the particular problem.

Analysis of current unemployment shows that, in brief:

1. The lines of work in which job opportunities have been declining most pronouncedly for some years are farming, mining, transportation, and the blue-collar crafts and trades in manufacturing industries.

2. The workers hardest hit have been the semi-skilled and the unskilled (along with inexperienced youths newly entering the labor market). These workers have accounted for a significant part of the increase in the level and duration of unemployment. Among white-collar groups, employment has continued to increase and unemployment has shown little change even in times of cyclical downturn.

3. The areas hardest hit have been, primarily, individual areas dependent upon a single industry, and cities in which such industries as autos, steel, and electrical equipment were heavily concentrated.

Actions best suited to helping these groups would appear to include more training and retraining to develop skills needed in expanding industries; provision of more and better information about job opportunities for various skills in various local labor markets; tax programs to stimulate investment that will expand work opportunities; re-

vision of pension and benefit plans to eliminate
penalties on employees moving to new jobs; reduction of impediments to entry into jobs, and so on.
Measures to alleviate distress and hardship are, of
course, imperative at all times.

In some of the instances cited, the primary obli-
gation of the Government will be leadership, rather
than action, for obviously a major responsibility
and role in efforts to overcome unemployment,
both cyclical and structural, rests upon management and labor.

For our part, we in the Federal Reserve intend
to do our share in combating the cyclical causes of
unemployment, as effectively as we can, and in
fostering the financial conditions favorable to
growth in new job opportunities.

Boiled down, Mr. Martin's excellent commentary
amounted to this:

(1) that structural unemployment will not give way to
noninflationary spending schemes, contrary to the as-
sertions of the spending school which is so entrenched
in official Washington these days; and (2) that "specific
actions" especially tailored to meet the "who," "where,"
and "why" of unemployment are indispensable.

In contrast, the Council of Economic Advisers believes that the massive spending approach to the unemployment question, which I regard as a holdover
from depression conditions, need not be inflationary.

What is as important, the Council is apparently prepared to risk inflation by way of such spending, though Mr. Kennedy's advisers admittedly do not put the matter quite so bluntly.

There is an interesting sequel to Mr. Martin's testimony on the unemployment problem.

Congressman Henry S. Reuss of Wisconsin was so concerned that he asked Mr. Martin if he would take another look at his own view and that of the Council. Not only did Chairman Martin do so, but if anything he made an even stronger statement in a carefully prepared reply to Congressman Reuss. The following is the relevant part of the restatement:

> The upward drift that unemployment has shown over recent economic cycles is a matter about which I expressed special concern. I noted that, among certain groups of workers and in certain geographical areas, unemployment had remained disturbingly large, even during periods of high-level activity. Unemployment of this type, is said to be structural in nature because it is associated, at least in part, with such factors as shifts in consumer demand, depletion of resources, shifts in defense activity, changes in technology, foreign competition, and relocation of plants. A major difficulty in absorbing into other gainful activity workers displaced by such developments is that their skill, education, training, and backgrounds

are not generally those required in expanding activities. In addition, mobility of workers attached to declining industries is limited because they often are middle-aged or other workers with families who have deep roots in their home communities.

In calling attention to the problems of structural unemployment, it was not at all my intention to suggest priorities in terms of remedial measures. I see no inconsistency in proposing that responsible policies be pursued simultaneously, on the one hand, to stimulate the economy, reverse the downdrift in economic activity, and decrease cyclical unemployment, and, on the other hand, to alleviate unemployment resulting from structural changes. Indeed, I believe that we should pursue both courses of action.

Certain forms of unemployment, as I tried to make clear in my statement, are not readily responsive to overall monetary and fiscal measures. Where causes of unemployment are due to special factors such as immobility of labor or inappropriate skills of workers, massive applications of monetary or fiscal stimulants after recovery is well under way could produce inflationary pressures without solving the more selective unemployment problems. Accordingly, it has seemed important to me that certain measures to assist those who suffer hardship because of dynamic structural changes should be considered along with steps taken to influence overall economic activity.

The Federal Reserve is to be congratulated for bringing the fundamental conflict of opinion out into the open. As a nation, the main hope we have for minimizing the risk of applying the wrong remedies is to have adequate public discussion of the issues, not only in the Congress but among interested citizenry across the land.

6. DOGMAS AND DISTRACTIONS

WHEN most Americans talk about their jobs, the ones they have, want, or may have lost, they usually do it privately with native good sense. Serious fathers tell their sons that they must not leave school too soon, lest they risk a lack of training which, almost inevitably these days, will be translated into a future lack of work. Serious trade union leaders may talk publicly about spreading the work, through restrictive work rules or artificially shortened hours, but many talk privately about their personal conviction that only retraining, job-skill improvements will do the job that really needs doing. Legislators, when they have time to contemplate the national welfare rather than local votes, will dwell on the same subjects.

At the level of public debate, however, there are vested emotions and notions that make straight and straightforward talk about America's jobs virtually impossible.

One of these which, admittedly, I have belabored is

57

the depression-born notion that public works, public spending are the only easy answers to unemployment. For our older generation this is an understandable hangover. For our younger people it is a new intoxication with the idea that life can be forever cradle-secure if only there is a public parent to replace the private ones that footed the bills through childhood.

There are other notions as meaningful, if not more so. One is the conscience-prodding complaint that we have weakened our economy (and, inferentially, our ability to have full employment) by overattention to the gimcracks and gewgaws of modern industry, to gadgets and tail-fins, to deodorants and costume jewelry rather than to "things that are good for people."

From this come the arguments that only strong and highly centralized government actually can protect the people from the monsters of Madison Avenue, with their wily snares and television commercials, and regulate the production and distribution of the "good things." Also from the same source rise the annual freshets of argument that the greedy private sector is gobbling up our substance while the public sector goes begging. Moreover, state and local governments are viewed as insufficient representatives of this public sector, thus focusing all need on the federal level.

Swirling from the steppes comes the argument that whereas Russia is growing like an arctic weed we are withering on the vine. And lacing it all together is the constant pressure to spend, spend, spend—with the federal government's tax power being conveniently substituted (easy payments, withholding, you'll never miss it if you don't get it, we only owe it to ourselves, etc.) for the accumulation of private savings, capital, that actually have always built the plants that housed the machines that gave us our jobs.

It is little wonder, with all those alarums and excursions on the stage, that the poor hero of the piece—the simple question of matching skills to available jobs—rarely gets a hearing.

I would, and many another legislator would also, much prefer to get on with the discussion of jobs and prosperity without having to battle the shouts from the special-interest ivory towers. Hopefully, this will be possible in the Congress before it is too late. Hopefully, the American people will get fed up with our national talking around the point and demand that we get down to cases.

Until then, however, the distractions must be at least covered lest there seem some void in the discussion, lest the amazingly simple situation in regard to employment and unemployment seem somehow unglamorous compared to the gaudy argumentation that has kept the subject from fully rational discussion so far.

First, it is simply not true that we have been starving the public sector. A glance at the facts shows just the contrary. For instance, social insurance grew almost

300 per cent from $5 billion to $19 billion between 1950 and 1960, a period in which the Gross National Product rose less than 80 per cent. Federal financing of research has expanded at an even greater rate, from $1 billion to $7 billion, though most of it admittedly was channeled into defense. And total educational outlay increased from $9 billion to $24 billion during the same period. As a life trustee of Dartmouth, I have particular interest in this area. I would be quite alarmed by any actual weakening of our educational system at any level. What are the facts? Nearly every component of educational outlay has shown substantial growth. The number of classrooms has been expanding so nicely that in the next decade we are even likely to develop a surplus. We are already almost in balance. And if President Kennedy's figure of classroom needs from 1960 to 1970 may be used—his estimate in the education message was put at 600,000 units—it is certain that the record will stump the so-called "experts." Mr. Kennedy's estimate of needs is at the rate of 60,000 classrooms a year. How does this compare with the recent record? The Office of Education records the nation's construction of classrooms from 1956 to 1961 at the annual average rate of 69,860 classrooms. This record of actual construction is almost 10,000 per year more than the yearly average asked for by the President. Regarding the assertion that we consume too many private gadgets, mainly

because our wants are artificially created by the advertising fraternity, there are also relevant facts.

For one thing, do people who first bought an article primarily because of advertising—or under the influence of advertising—relinquish the product once the advertising stops? The evidence shows that in many if not most cases people continue to buy previously advertised goods after they have been emancipated from the alleged advertising pressure. Finally, there are the attitudes of visitors to our shores from the underdeveloped nations. Most of them develop a taste for luxuries formerly unknown to them. The "anti-gadget" logic requires that they relinquish such newly acquired luxury standards on returning to their homeland, where (1) there is no so-called advertising pressure and (2) price levels are considerably lower than ours. What actually happens? In many instances, the foreigners, on returning home, continue to purchase goods for which they acquired a taste while in the United States, and they do so even in the face of considerable sacrifice.

If people's private wants are only artificially created, if additional private consumption adds almost nothing to human welfare, then it would be correct to hold that the loss of the production involved would also be inconsequential. In short, all of us really could do without our private consumption, or much of it! What we need, such a line attempts to prove, is less private consumption and more public services.

Writing in 1958, John Kenneth Galbraith "proved" that additional private production satisfied only unwanted wants. Therefore, he claimed, it would be almost foolish to pay attention to problems of efficiency in the private sector of the economy. That is, since he believed that satiety of wants prevails in the domain of private production, there would be no significant social loss if such production were carried on at less than maximum efficiency. Views such as these made quite an impression on the general reading public during the 1958 Congressional campaign. The ideas swayed some voters. Yet, at that very moment, although Dr. Galbraith was unaware of it, producers in the United States were beginning to feel the effect of a relative loss of productive efficiency as compared with competitors in other countries. The United States balance of payments had begun to deteriorate badly and, in 1960, the country actually witnessed a serious "gold scare" and a large loss of gold the like of which only old-timers could remember.

Yet, despite its economic naïveté, it is doubtful if any book in recent times has done so much as Galbraith's to propagate the idea that vast centralism in government is good for the country. Vast centralism is no mere abstraction: it means, concretely, vast taxes to pay for federal projects and undertakings, a slower rate of economic growth as resources are diverted into the bureaucracy, and delay in attending to many of our real national problems. Outstanding among the latter, of course, is that of coming to grips with effective ways of upgrading our work force, to the end that technological progress is not slowed because we have insufficient workers with modern skills.

Massive expenditures by the federal government also are alleged to be necessary because the states and localities are no longer able to carry their share of the load. In other words, if the units of government nearest the people cannot finance expanding local requirements, as alleged, federal finance must win by default.

President Kennedy's Council of Economic Advisers has asserted in response to a question which I had put to it that state and local finance has deteriorated. The Council's view rests on several propositions.

First, its pessimism respecting state and local finance is traceable to what it calls the relation between the demands on states and localities as the economy grows and what it chooses to label the *"automatic* responses of state and local revenues." The former grow faster than the latter, largely because the revenues derive mainly from what it calls relatively inflexible sources. Second, the Council of Economic Advisers holds that federal revenues necessarily increase faster than the general growth of the economy. Third, the Council is concerned about the expansion in the deficits and debts of states and localities. The deficits rose from an annual average of $400 million in the period 1948–50 to an average of $2 billion in 1958–60, while the debts increased from

$18.5 billion in 1948 to $67 billion in 1960. The Council admits, however, that the debt was incurred for sound purposes, and that it is matched by good assets.

In short, the President's Council of Economic Advisers accepts what the states and localities are doing, but fears their inability to continue doing so in the future. How do the Council's views stand up in relation to the record?

Its first proposition hinges on the idea that state and local revenues do not automatically respond to rising expenditures on the part of such units of government. But no one ever claimed that their revenues either do or necessarily have to respond automatically. The significant thing is that the local people vote to increase revenues when these are needed. They do so in an open manner, for items clearly labeled as to purpose. And they clearly identify the official who is doing the taxing in, say, the case of the property tax, which accounts for about half of state and local revenues. Such relationships are obscured in the field of sales and income taxes, especially those levied at the federal level. There is infinitely more care exercised in public spending when the taxpayer knows that he is paying a tax, what he is paying for, and who is taxing him.

The Kennedy Council of Economic Advisers attaches importance to the allegation that federal revenues increase faster than the rate of growth of the economy— and that, in consequence, federal spending should be given priority over state and local handling of many if not most governmental affairs. This way of putting the matter is only a restatement of the familiar—and erroneous—charge that the yield of the property tax (a mainstay of local finance) does not rise with the progress of the economy, but that the tax is stagnant, subject to statutory rate restrictions, and declining steadily in relative importance.

The opposite is true. This may be demonstrated by going to the record under reasonably normal conditions, say the long period up to the depression of the 1930's and the period since the last full wartime year of 1944. In both periods, property tax collections expanded at a faster rate than national income, and even more rapidly than the grand total of income, sales, and miscellaneous taxes. The property tax was stagnant only during the depression of the 1930's and during the Second World War. From 1944 to 1959, for example, property tax collections expanded by no less than 225 per cent, while all other taxes increased 90 per cent and the national income 118 per cent. The record reflects the little-known fact that our national wealth has been increasing in value at a faster rate than our national income. This alone should quiet the Council of Economic Advisers' concern over the growth of state and local debt. At any rate, that concern would be far more meaningful if it paid similar attention to the really big segment of our public debt—and to the federal spending policies which keep on pushing such debt skyward, without producing any of the wealth which, in turn, produces jobs.

Not only has the federal government hogged the taxes which enables it to "descend annually upon its taxpayers like a ton of bricks," but this very pattern of taxation has made it more difficult for other units of government to finance their budgetary needs. This fact, of course, is but another reason why the impressive revenue record of the states and localities is so significant.

The United States cannot avoid a fairly large federal government operation. We cannot largely because of military threats from the Communist empire, the need for attention to tendencies in parts of the free world which might involve a crumbling and disintegration of the social and political order, and the ever-changing challenges presented by our complex relations with allies in NATO, SEATO, and CENTO. Just keeping our military defenses modern and strong would make for a large central government operation, so big and costly is today's military establishment.

The piling of questionable spending programs on top of these really vital ones can only cause a great and perhaps dangerous dilution of national energies.

Recognition of this has even produced the irony of lectures by continental European officials on the need for Washington to put its fiscal house in order—in particular, the admonishing reminders made at the

Vienna meeting of the International Monetary Fund, of which we are the biggest single member. Thus, the French had us in mind when they lectured easy-spending nations on the need for "sound policy to ward off the recurrence of inflationary pressure." And the Germans emphasized the well-known principle that a workable international monetary order required "monetary discipline at home."

These nations had more than a mere academic interest in the economic health of the United States. They hold dollar balances in large quantities as part of their monetary reserves, and so have an enormous interest in measures to help protect the dollar.

There was a lot of irony in all this. Did not the United States for years, when the dollar was a strong currency, sternly lecture the Europeans on the need to put their fiscal house in order? We did so, to be sure, in an effort to avoid having them siphon off dollars from us when they were relatively undisciplined in spending. By the same logic, the Europeans would be reluctant to provide financial help to us in an emergency if, in a claimed effort to avoid financial crises, we really were not seriously trying to stay clear of easy spending policies of our own. Despite this, Congress has been solemnly told that we could push ahead with spending schemes without much fear of adverse consequences. Did we not, after all, have better brakes than ever before? We could always tame the economy by pressing on the monetary and fiscal brakes, should inflation threaten to get out of hand. This was the line taken by the Presidential economic advisers.

But it was not very reassuring. For one thing, as sober economists have emphasized, fiscal remedies are difficult to graft onto high-level budgets dominated by necessarily large defense expenditures. For another, the experience with bond pegging under another Democratic President convinced few that the same pegging school would allow the monetary brakes to be applied, unless too late in the day.

What was most feared, however, was that the free spenders would have to resort to direct controls over prices and wages, actions never previously taken in peacetime. Such a policy would destroy our free economy.

7. EXPORTING ERROR

AMERICANS have always been concerned by the problems of employment, not only at home, but abroad as well. Helping the underdeveloped nations to develop, as we have massively been doing since the end of the Second World War, is surely a reflection of this. It is often said that unless the standard of living of all peoples can be raised, our own will be constantly threatened.

This concern also has been a theoreticians' delight in affording opportunities to try spending techniques even more extreme than those acceptable to the American voter.

It was thought, apparently, that massive government spending could easily be rationalized for such countries —after all, did they not "need" roads, port facilities, irrigation projects, new schools, enlarged railway systems, electric power plants, steel mills, et al.? They needed, above all, massive doses of what was termed "social overhead capital" if the West was to have any chance of satisfying the so-called "revolution of rising expectations." Included in the priority was the alleged need for highly centralized planning schemes, to see to it that government investment in the area of "social overhead" occurred with a "big push" in the "correct" large amounts and in the "right places."

Full-blown theories were hatched, and new university courses offered in many an American institution of higher learning. We began to hear of such esoteric language as the "take-off," "preconditions for growth," "capital-output ratios," "investment coefficients," and all the rest.

The whole literary process kept the spending theorists busy, broadened the armory of their intellectual weapons, won them generous financial support from the giant foundations—and maintained the cutting edge of theoretical doctrines which might be used later on to influence the American voter himself in his own back yard.

In particular, such theoreticians fell in love with Indian socialism, with its multiyear development plans, its strong discrimination against even domestic Indian private capital in ideologically determined "key" industrial sectors, and its penchant for offering gratuitous moral advice to the United States and the West in connection with nearly every move undertaken by the West to stiffen resistance to Soviet imperialism. India's struggle against poverty did indeed strike a receptive cord in us. But we could not avoid the age-old problem of ends and means, especially in the light of the great record of the American free economy in overcoming its own "less developed" status of decades ago.

At any rate, even the then Senator Kennedy was sold on the "wisdom" of shoring up the financial side of Indian socialism. Though little known, Mr. Kennedy co-sponsored a Senate Resolution in 1958 and again in 1959, both defeated, that would have pledged enough taxpayer dollars to make India's socialist plans work. Interestingly enough, India's planning developed some very wasteful forms, despite the extreme human suffering in that land when waste occurs. There is, for example, the little-known situation concerning three new government-owned and operated million-ton steel mills which came into operation, by coincidence, just before President Kennedy assumed office.

The Indian planners assumed that the mills would run at full capacity as soon as completed. This facile assumption was made despite the fact that India had had little experience in large-scale steelmaking and had even fewer trained and tested plant managers. Actually, there were enough technical personnel to run the mills at only half capacity. Had investment in the mills been planned rationally, the way private investors do things, the three would have been phased in over a period of years so as to avoid waste of precious capital. How many millions of small Indian businessmen were denied foreign exchange by the Socialist authorities owing to

the commitments made in connection with poorly
planned government steel mills, only the future historian
will know. And how many productive jobs were thus
lost, in a nation desperately needing productive work
opportunities?

As mentioned, the two Senate Resolutions which Mr.
Kennedy cosponsored were defeated when put to a
vote. It was not so easy, of course, to defeat Mr. Kennedy after he had become President. He and his advisers went in for such innocuous-sounding ideas as
"comprehensive development plans" for newly emerging nations in the underdeveloped areas, in many of
which illiteracy was widespread and elementary aspects
of the democratic process were not even understood,
let alone practiced. Yet the President even proceeded
so far as to suggest that United States foreign aid dollars would be made conditional upon other nations taking the planned quasi-Socialist route to their economic
development.

Mr. Khrushchev, after discovering that many of his
subordinates were fiddling with the official government
figures on production, caustically remarked that "You
can't make pancakes out of statistics." He was right. And
his statement was important in a nation still relying
heavily on a backward diet of cereals. Because statistics
in Russia are a weapon in the cold war, there are few
data in the world whose reliability is so low. Nevertheless, since sputnik, Americans have not only been be-

lieving Russian statistics, but they have been using them to "prove" that the United States economy is failing to grow at a sufficiently rapid pace.

What are the facts about rates of growth? Before sputnik, it was commonplace to note the near-universality of praise for the growth-rate of the American economy as the marvel of the world. Writing in the early 1950's, for example, two acute students of our economy (Papandreou and Wheeler, *Competition and Its Regulation*) stated a simple truth when they observed that "the performance of our economy, especially during the last two decades, has been so impressive that even the difficult-to-please critics are willing to admit it."

Growth is not easy to measure. However, a handy statistic is widely used as a rough measure. This is the concept of Gross National Product, or the value of the nation's current production. Though not originally intended as a measure of growth, GNP is now so used for want of anything better. It has very serious implications, as I pointed out in 1961 on the floor of the House of Representatives: we must be wary of GNP as a measure of economic growth because there are so many imperfections or gaps in the data.

First, the compilation of GNP leaves many gaps of unmeasured economic activity. Only 35 per cent of American women, those in the labor force, have their work show up in GNP. The figure, in other words, does not reflect the work of housewives. Russia, largely because of her relative backwardness, has 63 per cent of her women in the labor force. Surely our housewives' time is real economic activity, but it does not show up in GNP, and thus we undermeasure as compared with Russia.

Our government's economic activity is not measured in an adequate way because we have no independently determined dollar value to attach to what the units of government do. Instead, we use a convention of measuring it in terms of the sums budgeted by the respective legislatures.

Many important activities go untabbed. For instance: all unpaid charity and religious work, all the vast amount of do-it-yourself activity which is so conspicuous in the United States, and all home study, research, and inventiveness which is undertaken without remuneration.

Increased efficiency or increased productivity show up as a *minus* factor in Gross National Product, whereas economic mistakes—in the form of useless or inefficient Russian hydroelectric plants such as the ones that Khrushchev has complained about—can loom large in "expanding" GNP for several years.

Finally, there is the case of military production, which generates so much obsolete and unused equipment. In the long run this does not represent real economic growth. Indeed, it may spell economic deterioration. We should realize that the Russian GNP is greatly exaggerated on this score, since as compared with the United States a very much larger percentage of Soviet GNP is accounted for by military outlays. The reader should also be reminded that these outlays have a tremendous real cost, since they come out of the hides of people who are forced by their government to do without a long list of highly desired consumer goods and services.

Our long-term economic growth rate has been at the rate of about 3.5 per cent a year. This rate rises a little during expansions, and falls somewhat during economic contractions. Moreover, inasmuch as the deficiency of our price statistics, on which the calculated growth rate is partly based, also has the effect of understating growth, our rate of increase in production is higher than indicated. However, lest a better than 3.5 per cent growth rate appears to be a modest figure, it should be clear that it results in a doubling of national output in well under a generation.

This rate of growth, moreover, has been achieved in the framework of a free society, in which consumers are sovereign and thus effectively control the composition of output. In particular, they dictate that most of our economic resources—apart from those taken by government through its exercise of the taxing power—be used to satisfy themselves as consumers, even if this means heavy concentration on consumer goods and services (where annual productivity gains are relatively low) rather than on standard industrial production and heavy equipment (where rates of increase in productivity are relatively high). Finally, the United States has a mature industrial-agricultural economy, long the world's leader, and a large measure of satisfaction is realized in the form of prized leisure—which, of course, is another valued element that does not show up in GNP data. Incidentally, the time which millions of Russians spend daily in queuing up for ordinary necessities is negative leisure, though of course the statistics do not make a deduction from GNP to account for this stark fact of Soviet life.

Russia, to be sure, reports a higher economic growth rate than ours. Perhaps its true size is on the order of 5 per cent, but we really can't be sure, partly because of what Khrushchev himself knows to be the fiddling with statistics that is so widespread in the Soviet Union. What does such a figure mean? The fact is that the experts are not sure themselves, since Moscow does not oblige with all the particulars necessary to check the numbers. Our people thus are forced to rely on a number of guesses with respect to big segments of Soviet GNP. And on such guesses we often base debates regarding the need for more central authority to "get our economy moving."

As the University of Virginia's Professor Warren Nutter has shown in a study being done for the National Bureau of Economic Research, the Soviet growth rate is of about the same order of magnitude as that realized during the last period of Czarist rule over a half century ago. (That rate, in turn, was heavily influenced by the relatively high rate of foreign private investment, mainly French and German, which occurred in Russia at that time.) Also, the dictatorship almost starves the consumer sector of the economy in order to use scarce resources for industrial and military production. The Soviets are developing from a low industrial base, so that substantial increments to output are relatively easy to achieve for a time. The Russians have been benefiting tremendously and without cost from the use of new production techniques developed at great research and scientific cost in the West. Before long, Russia will have to use more of her own resources to achieve her own native technological improvements.

Finally, Soviet economic growth is extremely uneven, itself the product of the dictatorial control over every phase of the economy and the nature of the system itself. In particular, nearly half of the people still labor in agriculture, where they barely hold level in production. In sharp contrast, only about 8 per cent of the United States labor force is in agriculture, and production is so great that we give much of it away to foreigners both to avoid holding excessive surpluses in our warehouses and for humanitarian purposes.

Still the post-sputnik concern for Russian military power and the higher reported Soviet growth rate is used to support charges of economic failure in the United States. But in economies so dissimilar, using a simple GNP yardstick—itself full of deficiencies— means using a rubber yardstick which each measurement "expert" can stretch to whatever preconceived length he chooses.

If allowance is made for the differences in the two economies, the past American showing is generally better, not worse, as many writers claim, than that of the Russians. In addition we are losing production because government policy is mistakenly predicated upon a poorly reasoned spending approach when what is needed are more direct measures of job upgrading and job adjustment.

There is still another variant of the poor America thesis, held by the President's Council of Economic Advisers. The idea is that the "American economy today is beset . . . with persistent slack in production and employment," and that we face a "problem of chronic slack in the economy."

On what grounds does the Council conclude that we have a "chronic slack" in our economy? It does so on the basis of a certain way of setting up the statistics of GNP. During political campaigns in our country it is common to start and end a statistical series with a particular President's term of office. Of course, such beginning and terminal dates are purely political, and thus have no special economic significance. President Kennedy's Council of Economic Advisers is more subtle than this.

What it did was to select an extremely good year, then measure both backwards and forwards from that year to show a "trend line." It then compared the adjusted GNP data for any recent year with this calculated line, to show the economy's potential output. Subtracting any year's actual figure from this potential is supposed to measure the "gap" or "slack."

The Council of Economic Advisers chose 1955 as the base. Unemployment was 4 per cent in that year. The Council regards that as a "reasonable target for full utilization of resources." But, as Professor Burns has indicated in a published reply to the Council, a similar 4 per cent rate was also observed in 1947 and in 1957. The economy, however, was not booming quite as much in either year as it was in 1955.

On top of this, it is necessary to select a yearly rate of growth for an economy making full use of its resources. The Council has selected a rate of 3.5 per cent a year for this purpose.

These two elements are all that the Council believes it needs for calculating a "gap" or "slack" in the American economy. Of the two choices, it is the base period which usually involves the real problems, since the 3.5 per cent growth rate appears to rest on a more or less acceptable foundation in history (though output may grow for a time at a rate above or below the 3.5 per cent figure).

As Professor Burns has emphasized, whether or not there is a gap depends mainly on the period selected. Thus the Council's gap for 1960 was put at $32 billion. If the second quarter of 1957 had been used by the President's economic advisers, however, the gap by the same system of measurement would have been reduced to $20 billion. That is, the mere selection of another base period would reduce the so-called gap by nearly 38 per cent. But this is not all. The really interesting conclusion, which shows the Council's essential arbitrariness, is drawn when we see what the results would be if the second quarter of 1947 had been used as the base—a period, as we have seen, which also had a 4 per cent unemployment rate. On this completely valid basis, using the Council's own method of reckoning, the alleged gap would have vanished and a "gap in reverse" —a "surplus of output"—of $2 billion would be shown. In short, the picture one gets following the Council's logic in each case, depends on the starting point selected for the exercise.

A clear conclusion emerges. Since the economy was well on the upswing at the time that the Council was fiddling with "gap" statistics, there was a real danger that new spending programs were being arranged to make their impact precisely when the economy was ad-

vancing without them. Time and again in the past that
kind of road map has directed traffic only to the never-
never land of inflation. It avoids, shamefully, the high
road to the pay-window of the better life our technology
should earn us.

8. WHAT GOVERNMENT CAN AND CAN'T DO

GOVERNMENT spending, pump priming, does not equip a single man with the skills required to take one of the many new jobs created by our advancing technology. It can buy time, but only individual training or retraining can "buy" any real guarantee of real work and real income.

To be sure, if government spending is carried far enough—through deficit financing after the regular tax route gets too rough—some persons with obsolete skills will manage to find work. It was the limited success of such massive spending during the deep and unique depression of the 1930's that still beguiles so many into thinking that the same medicine will work again today.

(The most vigorous advocate of spending to get us out of the depression, Great Britain's Lord John Maynard Keynes, soberly revised his thinking before his death and after seeing our recovery. His last paper, which appeared in 1946, shortly after his death, warned that his spending theories simply were not applicable in a modern economy facing not depression, but inflation. Unfortunately, his last testament has had nowhere near the publicity or promulgation of his earlier depression-days works. We have suffered successive classes of depression-minded, spending-oriented economics graduates as a tragic consequence, and Keynes's name has become both hallowed and anathema undeservedly.)

The time inevitably arrives, if a spending course is followed to solve employment problems, when there must be an accounting. For a time, under the impetus of massive federal spending, it is easier for industries in the technological van to sell their output at profitable prices and to minimize the spontaneous upgrading of skills on the part of the work force. The result is that not enough production develops in the advancing sectors of the economy and essentially unwanted output gets produced for inventory because rising prices create the illusion of continued sales at a profit. Worst of all, the spending philosophy really sidetracks government into essentially sterile activity. Washington with great fanfare takes the spending road, when the right route is in the wholly different direction of job escalation to meet the changing employment requirements of a dynamically growing economy.

Temporary excess capacity and unnecessarily high costs occur in the technologically advancing industries, in the sense that the most economic operations are not possible because there are insufficient workers with the right skills. Excessive inventories tend to be generated in the other industries, partly at the expense of an unnecessary rise in the price of raw materials absorbed in inventory building. Most of the excess inventory results from the lure of spending-induced increases in prices or anticipations of such increases. Finally, all the while only a minimal and unsystematic effort is made nationally to upgrade the work force, in consequence of which the economy remains saddled with an oversupply of outmoded skills and an undersupply of higher new ones.

Also, to the extent that labor unions or government policy maintain or increase the prices of oversupplied resources—as tends to happen when there is undue reliance on the spending medicine—the competitive international economic position of the United States actually deteriorates.

A positive theory is implicit in all this. Such a theory must be premised on a variety of more or less technical requirements, a suitable and rational articulation of procedures and systems for realizing such requirements, and government policies which induce the necessary action all along the economic front.

There are informational requirements that are of prime importance. What is the present and prospective pattern of industry expansion by significant industrial categories? What is the pattern of existing skill deficiencies by industry? By region? How are the deficit skills classified in terms of such considerations as man-months of required retraining? What is being done to equip existing members of the work force with such skills? By industry itself? By educational institutions, especially vocational? What kinds of estimation systems does business use? How might their results be aggregated on a current basis? These and other questions like them need to be answered.

Clearly, present and near-term requirements, minus present and prospective development of the necessary skills, equals the near-term unsatisfied requirements for job escalation.

The information needed is not mere reporting, such as occurs routinely in the compilation of much government data. The relevant context is a highly dynamic one, not the static variety involved in, say, collecting data on acreage sown to winter wheat. Considerable informational interchange is necessary, given the interrelations between job needs and the technical nature of new company processes on the front line of the dynamic economy. It must be remembered in this regard that there is a high research cost connected with the development of new products and production processes. This circumstance alone—the research cost and confidential nature of much of the information—probably dictates that a good part of job escalation will have to take place within the confines of the business firm, rather than by government—especially ponderous government at the national level. The implications with respect to the pattern of desired inducements and incentives are not hard to detect, at least in a general way. Job escalation certainly should not be bureaucratized!

In this connection, we hear little about the important successes in the area of job escalation which are being scored by individual business firms. Many companies have been able to make apprenticeship programs attractive to their bargaining unions. But it is the successes in retraining which have been most encouraging. Not all firms can do as well as IBM, which retrains some hundred thousand workers each year at a cost in millions, but a number are doing a fairly good job and could do much more under appropriate tax incentives and other government policies.

I am confident that the vast majority of companies should operate under a set of positive inducements respecting job escalation, so that they may do that which only private business can achieve well and efficiently in the best interest of the entire community.

Once we get moving along the job escalation front, however, we are sure to develop reasonably effective systems. Partly, this is because of the requirements for taking care of the great number of people who will be involved. Once begun, a strong momentum is sure to be generated, for men in all walks of life in effect will become parties to a great national effort. We will be engaged in a task of upgrading the work force by manageable small stages all along the line—teaching the ordinary laborer minor skills, equipping the semi-skilled with new techniques, and converting the skilled into advanced technicians.

I am optimistic about such an effort. Basically, this optimism is grounded in the great strides with which management science is moving ahead, and especially in the extent and intimacy of technical co-operation between practicing business management and our educational institutions. Moreover, the modern electronic computer is sure to help. My optimism is tempered by one fear: that our nation may continue to be sidetracked by the false cures of federal spending. Those who prescribe such a cure can also use government computers to crank out numbers in support of policy measures which are as shaky fundamentally as the spending cure itself.

It is in the field of government policy, and particularly in regard to the risk of bureaucratic meddling and the imposition of governmental barriers to a rational system of job escalation, that much thought is required of us all. The working man and private industry are sure to benefit immeasurably from a good system of job escalation. The former's effort will be rendered more productive, and his remuneration will rise accordingly. In fact, worker expectations alone should create positive self-generating forces of great significance. For its part, business management will clearly benefit from a system which keeps the work force geared in skill to the changing needs of modern technology. The lift to national economic efficiency will also aid the United States balance of payments.

But the case of the federal government is different, I fear. This is mainly because so many bureaus find their very reason for being tied to spending programs, and many appeals are likely to continue to be made to the voters in such terms. Contemporary Washington has a huge vested interest in the sheer effort of keeping spending going.

Washington's attitude does not, however, present an insurmountable barrier. The fallaciousness of the spending cure is, after all, a demonstrable thing, if only this fall-out of fallacies can be revealed to a wide audience. Then the ground will be laid for reaching the voter with a positive program. If, for example, the average man is simply told that automation reduces jobs, which only lavish spending can make good, I am afraid that the spending cure will retain its persuasiveness with many Americans. Unfortunately, false ideas about automation appear almost daily. As this is being written, for instance, a widely syndicated business columnist presents an all-too-common one-sided picture, namely, that a great many jobs will be lost in the United States in the current year because of automation. When such writing includes not a word about the important fact that automation is also responsible for most of our new job opportunities, there is a violation of the elementary rules of fairness. Such writing also ignores well-recorded and very relevant facts. We all know that automation has been substantial in the last two decades, for example. Yet manufacturing payrolls increased by 52 per cent in this period, employment in the wholesale and retail trade jumped 67 per cent, service employment grew by 86 per cent, and jobs in contract construction expanded 102 per cent. Consider a single example: despite the use of dial equipment, the Bell Telephone System has expanded its employment from two hundred thousand to six hundred thousand since 1920. I have even heard it said that with the current volume of telephone use, the absence of dialing would so expand the demand for old-fashioned telephone operators that nearly every female entrant into the labor force would have to pitch in just to meet the requirements for telephone service!

Despite my concern for a let-the-government-do-it attitude regarding job escalation, I do not rule out government. In fact, government at all levels has an important role to play in a well-designed program of job escalation. There is, for instance, the Manpower Retraining Act, the broad outlines of which were formed in the work of the Joint Economic Committee. (The text of this vital step toward an improved employment climate appears as an appendix to this book.) Our federal tax laws, for another instance, have been written as if the upgrading problem did not even exist. Such laws discourage labor mobility and in effect penalize or provide no positive inducements for job retraining programs in most of industry. (In the next chapter I shall suggest specific changes in our tax laws which will have to be made if the nation is to develop a sound program of rapid job escalation.) Our state-administered unemployment compensation systems are so operated today that they make only a minimal contribution to the ungrading of skills, though they are capable of assisting to an important degree if we had the wisdom to adopt a sound general framework for policy. The Labor Department and the Department of Health, Education and Welfare barely know the problem exists.

Finally, there is the sphere of local-government activity in behalf of job escalation. Outstandingly important in this area is the role of our educational institutions. This is a truly major field of skill-development enterprise in our society, which the University of Chicago's Professor Theodore W. Schultz, in his recent presidential address to the American Economic Association, has aptly called "investment in human capital." Though I maintain that our nation (1) does not adequately appreciate how changing job requirements stem from our dynamically growing economy and (2) is still under the spell of hypnotic spending, I do not for a moment underrate the contributions of our educational system. It is through this system, in the main, that our people "invest in themselves" and, in Schultz's fine words, "enlarge the range of choice available to them."

An emphasis on upgrading is, I submit, in keeping with the noble process of "enlarging the range of choice" which has been so important in proving strength for our free society. The point I keep emphasizing boils down, of course, to the need to accelerate our efforts in this field if we are to meet the skill requirements of our dynamic economy. This does not call for scattering our spending shots all over the national landscape, but for targeting them carefully as in the field of education, where so much constructively co-operative work has long been achieved in close association with local industry, business, and labor. Through an extension of such co-operation there can be created the skills which mean jobs for all who want them.

9. BASIS FOR A PROGRAM

OUR dynamic economy has created a demand for so many skills of so many new and different sorts that we have, in amazing fact, developed large larbor shortages. This is the crux of the so-called unemployment problem: not the lack of jobs, but the lack of skills to fill available jobs. This is the growing pain of our economy—it is not the fatal sickness of a sick economy, as those who see only the "job wanted" but never the "help wanted" columns of our papers so often say.

Most of the unfilled job requirements are known only in general terms, however.

We need many more engineers, in old as well as altogether new fields. We need more doctors, more nurses, more garage mechanics, more lab technicians, more scientists of all sorts, more teachers with more and varied training, more salesmen with genuine technical expertise about their complex products, more management technicians, more computer operators, more computer designers, more computer programmers, more highly skilled production workers. More, more, and still more, as each new wave of skills breeds the machines and the services that demand ever more skills and creates ever more jobs in new fields.

Newspapers are filled with advertising for needed skills. Many employers no longer use such columns because their experience has shown that the necessary skills simply are not available. In such cases they undertake to train people to fill these jobs.

What is more, the skill requirements of our dynamic economy are snowballing. The Department of Labor recently estimated that about five thousand new job titles will be added to its dictionary of occupational titles in the decade of the sixties. During the same period some 8 per cent to 10 per cent of current job titles will become obsolete.

Since technological growth and heads-up, innovating management create a demand for more jobs than they make obsolete, our basic task as a nation is to find the ways to meet such a demand.

The cost, surprisingly in the age of so much federal spending, is bound to be relatively low and in a sense self-liquidating. Work at higher skills obviously pays more, which enlarges the tax base, other things being equal. Also, success in this endeavor will reduce the incentive for featherbedding, which fear of technological unemployment frequently generates. The resulting greater productivity will also serve to expand the tax base. Then, billions now spent in all manner of government programs to conceal unemployment in the fog of inflation could be saved and federal taxes accordingly cut to the bone.

A successful attack on employment even gives great promise of increasing a general understanding of the role of government in our society. Government is ancillary, a handmaiden of the private sector. Government is not a copartner of the people. It is their servant, and government jobs are created only when individuals in their private enterprise create a demand for ancillary assistance. This, and not the state concept of government as a big spender, should guide us in the era ahead.

Of all the things that government might be tempted to do in finding answers to job problems, the most necessary first step is to satisfy requirements for relevant information about emerging skill requirements as well as about the pattern of unneeded skills. We must upgrade skills across the land, but "upgrade for what?"

1. Urgently necessary are answers based on an analytical, nationwide study of the skills of the future, emerging skills of the present, and obsolescent skills of the past. Such answers are needed, negatively, lest we retrain men, as we are unfortunately doing today in some instances, for outmoded or unneeded skills, and, affirmatively, to steer our efforts in the right direction on a time basis.

2. To this end, there should be established a national

clearinghouse for the classification of these skills and their needs on a geographic basis. At present, a limited amount of work is being done in this area by the Bureau of Labor Statistics and the United States Employment Service. But these agencies overlap a good deal, and their operations do not synchronize well with large segments of private activity bearing on the subject.

3. The clearinghouse system should aim to present, on a timely and co-ordinated basis, all relevant public and private information, bearing mainly on skill requirements in relation to existing and near-term supplies of trained manpower. This information should be suitably classified as to levels of remuneration by skill categories, length of retraining periods for typical upgrading situations, and the like.

Co-ordination with vocational and other educational institutions would be necessary in order that the various interrelated activities be reflected in the clearinghouse's reports and analyses.

4. Such information, moreover, should be systematically used by the country's Armed Forces, especially in connection with their work in vocational guidance, since these services occupy a strategic position in relation to job escalation and career planning for many young people.

5. The clearinghouse system and co-operative work by many local groups in connection with it should play a constructive role also in education. The point is worth stressing, since the country's increasing emphasis on rapid technological improvement has vast implications for educational policy.

6. Primarily, we should pay relatively less attention to old-fashioned narrow training, and place more emphasis in the schools on fundamental subjects. For it is the basic subjects which provide the future working population with a strong springboard to sound skill in youth plus improvement and occupational flexibility after they have entered the labor force. Much of this is known, of course. What a skill clearinghouse system could do in particular would be to create a framework within which citizens could more actively co-operate with school authorities in weeding out obsolete courses and programs and in helping to expedite the upgrading of teachers.

A clearinghouse system could also exert pressure on behalf of school administrators who now might lack strong local support for reforms. For instance, in a great number of vocational schools, or the vocational departments of regular schools, students needing discipline are dumped into, say, the machine shop course. This simply disrupts the course, and class effectiveness suffers badly as a result. Why should disciplinary requirements and methods curtail necessary skill development?

7. At the college level, including both the two-year junior college and the regular undergraduate institutions, upgrading of curricula and instruction also seems to be

necessary in many cases if the nation is to achieve a maximum pace of job escalation in technical and professional work. College officials, to be sure, are doing more than before in an effort to improve effectiveness. A functioning skill clearinghouse system could constructively enhance their work.

Especially worthy of study and close attention is the tendency to lengthen college programs in many states, ostensibly to improve the student product. Educational history shows that the usual result is little more than course proliferation, with many low-quality offerings remaining in curricula instead of being displaced by more substantial and useful ones. With a good clearinghouse system, responsible local pressure can be brought to bear in support of those educators who are fighting within their institutions for stronger courses that genuinely challenge students coming from improved high schools. This work is important and by its nature needs to be done chiefly at the local level. Today's needs for well-educated people are such that a college degree is equivalent in importance, and general need and availability, to the high school diploma of only a generation or so ago.

The significance is well illustrated in a study prepared by Professor Almarin Phillips of the University of Virginia. He estimates that no less than 40 per cent of the increase in our total national production is associated with technological change. Professor Phillips adds significantly that this change is now more rapid, but not materially different from change in previous periods. The problems developed not so much from the changes as from the failure of business, labor, and government to recognize them at their outset, when merely marginal corrections will suffice to keep skills and needs in step.

Such corrections, it should be emphasized, can be most effectively made, first of all, at the community level. The measure of their effectiveness, in fact, might well be the degree to which they prevent problems from ascending the scale of complexity to the regional, state, or federal levels.

Where better, for instance, to spot and prepare solutions for technological changes than at the level of the community in which the changes first begin to affect individual employees and managements? Community educational institutions can be and must be more sensitive to such changes. Management, as it plans ahead, should be a partner in such community efforts—never excluded from them. The responsibility goes two ways, of course. Management must not exclude itself.

For the community that fails in its response to these challenges, preferring to pass the buck to higher, distant levels of government, there is an obvious and terrible fate: dependency, loss of local pride and initiative, and, eventually, loss of citizens and a slow decline to blight.

10. POWERING THE PROGRAM

THERE ARE five broad areas in which action should be taken on the federal level to remove impediments to job escalation in the private sector of the economy.

As might be expected, revision of our tax laws must play an important part in this effort. As a member of the tax-writing Ways and Means Committee of the House of Representatives, I am acutely aware of the importance of tax policy for an effective nation-wide program of job escalation. It has been said with much truth that our tax laws are now all but blind on these matters.

The five areas for action, with my specific recommendations in each area, are as follows:

1. Tax laws, for instance, provide no personal incentive for individuals contemplating retraining. Cases are covered in our newspapers constantly showing how tax laws impede the very upgrading process that our country so badly needs to encourage. Note the following press account:

An Army captain got leave from his post as an artillery instructor to complete courses in psychology, public administration and history. Under an Army plan to encourage higher education of its personnel, he continued to draw his regular pay, but he had to pay the added school expenses himself. The Internal Revenue Service, asked if the captain could deduct these outlays as an educational expense, said no. The law permits a deduction for costs of improving one's skills in an existing job, but not for those incurred to qualify for a new post.

Clearly, this shows that our tax laws work precisely to impede—not help—job escalation. Many individuals who want to improve their position know that they have to qualify for a *different* job to get a better one. The tax laws should reflect this elementary fact of life. Tax deductions or credits should be given to men and women who want to train for greater skill or competence.

2. Another way in which our tax laws hinder employment is the area of geographic labor mobility. The tax laws were written when only a relatively small percentage of our people owned their own homes, and when few persons sought work far beyond reasonable commuting distance from their normal place of residence. Today, however, it makes no sense to have our tax laws continue to regard a man's "legal residence" for tax purposes as the place where he works, for today

nearly 70 per cent of our people own their own homes and are not going to pull up family stakes just to enable the breadwinner to accept a challenging but perhaps temporary job two hundred miles away. Why should shortages of skills exist in sections of our country when men are prepared to work there temporarily if they are not penalized taxwise? The acceptance of such employment should not require that the workers relocate their entire family near the job site in such cases.

A realistic program for job escalation, therefore, would call for more realistic tax regulations defining "place of residence" as the "tax home" of those workers temporarily engaged in an occupation in another part of the country.

Together, these two tax reforms could do much directly to stimulate the more rapid skill development and job mobility that is necessary for the smooth performance of our dynamic economy.

3. The nation's unemployment insurance system also has a great potential as a vehicle for promoting the upgrading of our labor force. This system is paid for by private employers but administered by the states, with some participation by the federal government. It has achieved fairly good results in terms of providing stopgap financial assistance to men out of work, tiding them over the cyclical downswings. But little has been made of the system with respect to the challenge of upgrading the skills of the labor force.

There is a simple key to the needed reform of our unemployment compensation system as far as job escalation is concerned. It is found by answering this question: How is an unemployed person treated at present if he enrolls in a training school to learn a new or better skill? The answer is that he is removed from the unemployment rolls, and thus becomes ineligible for unemployment insurance benefits, in forty of the fifty states.

This is precisely the opposite of the policy that is called for. An unemployed person should be removed from the unemployment rolls if he cannot get a job in his obsolete skill and he *refuses* to start learning a skill that is in demand.

State legislation, therefore, should permit those engaged in training and retraining programs to continue to receive unemployment benefits up to normal amounts and limits, as is currently the case in only eighteen of our fifty states and the District of Columbia.

Moreover, there is a potential for job escalation in the broadening of merit rating in unemployment payments. The cost of unemployment insurance to individual employers varies with the employment record of the firm. In other words, companies experiencing heavy unemployment pay more than those with a record of little unemployment.

There is no incentive stemming directly from the operation of the unemployment insurance system to provide retraining for unemployed personnel. An unemployed worker who may be undergoing company-sponsored retraining is still classified as unemployed, and the firm's merit-rating suffers accordingly. Surely this makes little sense in view of the great need for increasing retraining opportunities.

States should broaden merit rating concepts to include on-the-job retraining, to the end that the employer is not penalized for extending this opportunity to his workers. This would be another step in the direction of rapid job escalation.

4. In our rapidly growing economy, machinery becomes *obsolete* before it wears out. This is the reality of our technological advancement. Do our tax laws reflect this reality? Not at all. We find, on an examination of the situation, that our tax laws are geared to the old economics of wear, not of obsolescence. Such tax machinery simply does not mesh with modern industrial requirements.

In spite of the long-needed recent revision of depreciation schedules, the problem remains. We do not yet know whether these new schedules will be responsive to the needs of the economy. Depreciation schedules must be kept up-to-date continually to reflect the economic reality of useful life.

It takes more investment money to buy machinery when it becomes obsolescent long before it wears out. For the sake of progress, therefore, one would think that our tax laws would encourage such investment. Yet cutting off such investment is precisely what our tax laws do. The lag in depreciation allowances is now estimated to be some $4 to $6 billion behind replacement needs. Our economic progress is obviously slowed down when a third of our industrial plant is obsolete, as it is today.

Our tax laws must permit more realistic depreciation allowances. We need this not only for the sake of more and better jobs in the United States, but also to keep the American economy competitive internationally and to impart strength to the dollar as a world currency. Today, for example, Britain allows more than 40 per cent depreciation on new machinery in the year of acquisition. Germany permits a write-off of 25 per cent the first year and about 58 per cent of the cost in the first three years. France does even better. We do only a fraction as well.

There are four overriding reasons why we must modernize tax legislation bearing on depreciation. First, we will experience an increase in the annual additions to our labor force in the next decade. Some three million new workers will be wanting productive jobs. Second, the investment cost per job—the amount required to create a new position—is rising, and is now between $20,000 and $25,000 per man. Third, there is a high investment cost in generating new products. Sensational as it is in fact, the pace of new product development is little known. Actually, about 30 per cent of the goods on the market today were not there only five years ago. Finally, our tax legislation respecting depreciation needs modernization to assure that the American economy remains up-to-date as compared with rival trading nations, especially in Europe.

The needed tax legislation should be in the form of generally applicable rates, known in advance to business management so that it can make the right kind of long-range investment plans. A system lodging discretionary authority with the government, adjusting depreciation rates or tax credits in terms of untested theoretical considerations—such as President Kennedy proposed shortly after assuming office—simply will not do the job.

5. Sound employment legislation also demands a well-ordered operation in the Congress of the United States. At present, this is lacking. There is overlapping jurisdiction among Congressional committees dealing with employment. Consider, for example, the way the subject of automation is handled in the House of Representatives. It is dealt with by the Education and Labor Committee, the Banking and Currency Committee, the Ways and Means Committee, and the Joint Economic Committee. Knowledge remains un-co-ordinated, and one committee usually acts without knowing very much about the experience of the other committees.

In this connection, I welcome the endorsement of the House Republican Policy Committee, for my proposal to establish a new co-ordinating committee. This would be a standing committee on employment, composed of members from each of the four committees mentioned in the preceding paragraph. Such a standing committee could recommend positive policies in the area of employment, co-operate with state legislatures and city councils throughout the country, and analyze Executive Branch activities in the economic field.

With faith in ourselves, and perserverance in job escalation without federalization, we can succeed in attaining a future of full employment. We can do so while strengthening our freedom, not through decisions which trickle down from an apex of authority in Washington but from actions originating in the broad base of the pyramid of America's economic and political strength—in the heart and soul of a strong and free people.

APPENDIX I

Some Hard Realities

SOME members of the labor force have rather limited opportunities for job development for reasons beyond their control.

The blind fall in this category. Though such individuals are now able to do more than was once the case, they face real handicaps in the job market, as everyone knows. It takes them much longer, as a rule, to prepare for a skilled task. Adjustment to new patterns of skill needs is thus far more costly and time-consuming than for most others. More serious, however, is the fact that the blind are forced to limit themselves to a rather restrictive list of job opportunities.

The case of the blind is so special that it may be desirable to use extraordinary measures in dealing with it. Perhaps we may want to reverse the job adjustment process that is required in a dynamic economy. For the blind, we may want to fit the job to the man rather than fit the man to the changing pattern of job needs. This can be done without broad social ill effects if the qualifying group is relatively small in number and, of course, because its members do labor under a special handicap which every normal American clearly recognizes. But it must be done in the spirit of voluntarism, not by government order.

Employers could reserve for the blind certain categories of work in their plants. How this might be done should be left to management, to assure that the most flexible possible arrangements are made. Little more need be said in general terms. Labor unions and the public surely would support management decisions in this area.

Other hard realities of upgrading the nation's labor force are revealed by the experience of Armour and Company when it closed its plant in Oklahoma City, laying off 400 employees. To help them, the Oklahoma Employment Service offered unemployment tests and counseling. Only 170 of the 400 workers took advantage of the Service's help or of the company's retraining program. Of the 170, only 60 gave evidence of being able to benefit from a retraining program.

One should not try to draw too many conclusions from this case, because only broadly based experience can support definitive conclusions. For example, one pattern of results might be observed if a person views the Armour case in isolation, while a different—and much more favorable—pattern might be expected if a broad cross-section of American industry were induced by appropriate tax and other incentives to offer a great variety of retraining programs to workers who were desirous of upgrading themselves.

One point, however, should be made about the Armour experience. Only a third of the displaced employees who availed themselves of tests and counseling gave evidence to the Oklahoma Employment Service that they could benefit from additional training. What about the other two thirds? Usually in cases of this kind the educational and aptitude levels do much to explain why some people are unlikely to benefit from efforts to upgrade themselves. Failure to complete elementary school, for example, can be a very serious handicap. The lack of a high school education may also be restrictive.

Individuals with a low I.Q. are likely to constitute quite a problem. This is the group which is least capable of benefiting from additional education, viewing the problem in its long-term dimensions. Short-run prospects with respect to job upgrading are also relatively unpromising in the case of such a group. The outlook, nevertheless, is better the more general the nation's effort in job development and redevelopment.

In this ascend-the-ladder process, even those with limited capacity for self-improvement find better job opportunities available to them. The key factor is the existence of a general movement, in which a large cross-section of the nation's labor force is actively engaged in job escalation.

Another of the hard realities that job upgrading musı face is that of the Negro worker.

As has been revealed recently in hearings before a subcommittee of the House Committee on Education and Labor, a number of unions are effectively blocking Negroes from receiving apprentice training.

Ex-President Conant of Harvard has even said that it is often more difficult for a Negro to gain admission to a union-controlled apprenticeship program than it is to get into the most selective medical school.

In this case, too, however, much depends upon the presence or absence of a *general effort,* characterized by vigor and drive, directed toward the rapid upgrading of the nation's work force. The mere existence of such an effort is bound to make all manner of objectionable practices stand out like sore thumbs. And there is no reason to believe that those who deny apprenticeship opportunities to Negroes will not sense their wrong-doing to a greater degree once the nation embarks on a vigorous national upgrading program.

APPENDIX II

Major Provisions of the
Manpower Development and Training Act of 1962

THE Congress finds that there is critical need for more and better trained personnel in many vital occupational categories, including professional, scientific, technical, and apprenticeable categories; that even in periods of high employment, many employment opportunities remain unfilled because of the shortages of qualified personnel; and that it is in the national interest that current and prospective manpower shortages be identified and that persons who can be qualified for these positions through education and training be sought out and trained, in order that the Nation may meet the staffing requirements of the struggle for freedom. The Congress further finds that the skills of many persons have been rendered obsolete by dislocations in the economy arising from automation or other technological developments, foreign competition, relocation of industry, shifts in market demands, and other changes in the structure of the economy; that Government leadership is necessary to insure that the benefits of automation do not become burdens of widespread unemployment; that the problem of assuring sufficient employment opportunities will be compounded by the extraordinarily rapid growth of the labor force in the next decade, particularly by the entrance of young people into the labor force, that improved planning and expanded efforts will be required to assure that men, women, and young people will be trained and available to meet shifting employment needs; that many persons now unemployed or underemployed, in order to become qualified for reemployment or full employment must be assisted in providing themselves with skills which are or will be in demand in the labor market; that the skills of many persons now employed are inadequate to enable them to make their maximum contribution to the Nation's economy; and that it is in the national interest that the opportunity to acquire new skills be afforded to these people in order to alleviate the hardships of unemployment, reduce the costs of unemployment compensation and public assistance, and to increase the Nation's productivity and its capacity to meet the requirements of the space age. It is therefore the purpose of this Act to require the Federal Government to appraise the manpower requirements and resources of the Nation, and to develop and apply the information and methods needed to deal with the problems of unemployment resulting from automation and technological changes and other types of persistent unemployment.

EVALUATION, INFORMATION, AND RESEARCH

To assist the Nation in accomplishing the objectives of technological progress while avoiding or minimizing individual hardship and widespread unemployment, the Secretary of Labor shall—

(1) evaluate the impact of, and benefits and problems created by automation, technological progress, and other changes in the structure of production and demand on the use of the Nation's human resources; establish techniques and methods for detecting in advance the potential impact of such developments; develop solutions to these problems, and publish findings pertaining thereto;

(2) establish a program of factual studies of practices of employers and unions which tend to impede the mobility of workers or which facilitate mobility, including but not limited to early retirement and vesting provisions and practices under private compensation plans; the extension of health, welfare, and insurance benefits to laid-off workers; the operation of severance pay plans; and the use of extended leave plans for education and training purposes. A report on these studies shall be included as a part of the Secretary's report required under section 104;

(3) appraise the adequacy of the nation's manpower development efforts to meet foreseeable manpower needs and recommend needed adjustments, including methods for promoting the most effective occupational utilization of and providing useful work experience and training opportunities for untrained and inexperienced youth;

(4) promote, encourage, or directly engage in programs of information and communication concerning manpower requirements, development, and utilization, including prevention and amelioration of undesirable manpower effects from automation and other technological developments and improvements of the mobility of workers; and

(5) arrange for the conduct of such research and investigations as give promise of furthering the objectives of this Act.

SKILL AND TRAINING REQUIREMENTS

The Secretary of Labor shall develop, compile, and make available, in such manner as he deems appropriate, information regarding skill requirements, occupational outlook, job opportunities, labor supply in various skills, and employment trends on a National, State, area, or other appropriate basis which shall be used in the educational, training, counseling, and placement activities performed under this Act.

MANPOWER REPORT

The Secretary of Labor shall make such reports and recommendations to the President as he deems appropriate pertaining to manpower requirements, resources, use, and training; and the President shall transmit to the Congress within sixty days after the beginning of each regular session (commencing with the year 1963) a report pertaining to manpower requirements, resources, utilization, and training.

GENERAL RESPONSIBILITY

In carrying out the purposes of this Act, the Secretary of Labor shall determine the skill requirements of the economy, develop policies for the adequate occupational development and maximum utilization of the skills of the Nation's workers, promote and encourage the development of broad and diversified training programs, including on-the-job training, designed to qualify for employment the many persons who cannot reasonably be expected to secure full-time employment without such training, and to equip the Nation's workers with the new and improved skills that are or will be required.

SELECTION OF TRAINEES

The Secretary of Labor shall provide a program for testing, counseling, and selecting for occupational training under this Act those unemployed or underemployed persons who cannot reasonably be expected to secure appropriate full-time employment without training. Whenever appropriate the Secretary shall provide a special program for the testing, counseling, and selection of youths, sixteen years of age or older, for occupational training and further schooling. Workers in farm families with less than $1,200 annual net family income shall be considered unemployed for the purpose of this Act.

Although priority in referral for training shall be extended to unemployed persons, the Secretary of Labor shall, to the maximum extent possible, also refer other persons qualified for training programs which will enable them to acquire needed skills. Priority in referral for training shall also be extended to persons to be trained for skills needed within, first, the labor market area in which they reside and, second, within the State of their residence.

The Secretary of Labor shall determine the occupational training needs of referred persons, provide for their orderly selection and referral for training under this Act, and provide counseling and placement services to persons who have completed their training, as well as follow-up studies to determine whether the programs provided meet the occupational training needs of the persons referred.

Before selecting a person for training, the Secretary shall determine that there is a reasonable expectation of employment in the occupation for which the person is to be trained. If such employment is not available in the area in which the person resides, the Secretary shall obtain reasonable assurance of such person's willingness to accept employment outside his area of residence.

The Secretary shall not refer persons for training in an occupation which requires less than two weeks training, unless there are immediate employment opportunities in such occupation.

The duration of any training program to which a person is referred shall be reasonable and consistent with the occupation for which the person is being trained.

Upon certification by the responsible training agency that a person who has been referred for training does not have a satisfactory attendance record or is not making satisfactory progress in such training absent good cause, the Secretary shall forthwith terminate his training and subsistence allowances, and his transportation allowances except such as may be necessary to enable him to return to his regular place of residence after termination of training, and withdraw his referral. Such person shall not be eligible for such allowances for one year thereafter.

TRAINING ALLOWANCES

The Secretary of Labor may, on behalf of the United States, enter into agreements with States under which the Secretary of Labor shall make payments to such States either in advance or by way of reimbursement for the purpose of enabling such States, as agents for the United States, to make payment of weekly training allowances to unemployed persons selected for training pursuant to the provisions of section 202 and undergoing such training in a program operated pursuant to the provisions of this Act. Such payments shall be made for a period not exceeding fifty-two weeks, and the amount of any such payment in any week for persons undergoing training, including uncompensated employer-provided training, shall not exceed the amount of the average weekly unemploment compensation payment (including allowances for dependents) for a week of total unemployment in the State making such payments during the most recent quarter for which such data are available: *Provided however,* That in any week an individual who, but for his training, would be entitled to unemployment compensation in excess of such allowance, shall receive an allowance increased by the amount of such excess. With respect to Guam and the Virgin Islands the Secretary shall by regulation determine the amount of the training allowance to be paid any eligible person taking training under this Act.

With respect to any week for which a person receives unemployment compensation under title XV of the Social Security Act or any other Federal or State unemployment compensation law which is less than the average weekly unemployment compensation payment (including allowances for dependents) for a week of total unemployment in the State making such payment during the most recent quarter for which such data are available, a supplemental training allowance may be paid to a person eligible for a training allowance under this Act. This supplemental training allowance shall not exceed the difference between his unemployment compensation and the average weekly unemployment compensation payment referred to above.

For persons undergoing on-the-job training, the amount of any payment which would otherwise be made by the Secretary of Labor under this section shall be reduced by an amount which bears the same ratio to that payment as the number of compensated hours per week bears to forty hours.

The Secretary of Labor is authorized to pay to any person engaged in training under this title, including compensated full-time on-the-job training, such sums as he may determine to be necessary to defray transportation and subsistence expenses for separate maintenance of such persons when such training is provided in facilities which are not within commuting distance of their regular place of residence: *Provided,* That the Secretary in defraying such subsistence expenses shall not afford any individual an allowance exceeding $35 per week, at the rate of $5 per day; nor shall the Secretary authorize any transportation expenditure exceeding the rate of 10 cents per mile.

The Secretary of Labor shall pay training allowances

only to unemployed persons who have had not less than three years of experience in gainful employment and are either heads of families, or heads of households as defined in the Internal Revenue Code of 1954, except that he may pay training allowances at a rate not exceeding $20 a week to youths over nineteen but under twenty-two years of age where such allowances are necessary to provide them occupational training, but not more than 5 per centum of the estimated total training allowances paid annually under this section may be paid to such youths.

After June 30, 1964, any amount paid to a State for training allowances under this section, or as reimbursement for unemployment compensation under subsection (h), shall be paid on condition that such State shall bear 50 per centum of the amount of such payments.

No training allowance shall be made to any person otherwise eligible who, with respect to the week for which such payment would be made, has received or is seeking unemployment compensation under title XV of the Social Security Act or any other Federal or State unemployment compensation law, but if the appropriate State or Federal agency finally determines that a person denied training allowances for any week because of this subsection was not entitled to unemployment compensation under title XV of the Social Security Act or such Federal or State law with respect to such week, this subsection shall not apply with respect to such week.

A person who refuses, without good cause, to accept training under this Act shall not, for one year thereafter, be entitled to training allowances.

Any agreement under this section may contain such provisions (including, as far as may be appropriate, provisions authorized or made applicable with respect to agreements concluded by the Secretary of Labor pursuant to title XV of the Social Security Act) as will promote effective administration, protect the United States against loss and insure the proper application of payments made to the State under such agreement. Except as may be provided in such agreements, or in regulations hereinafter authorized, determinations by any duly designated officer or agency as to the eligibility of persons for weekly training allowances under this section shall be final and conclusive for any purposes and not subject to review by any court or any other officer.

If State unemployment compensation payments are paid to a person taking training under this Act and eligible for a training allowance, the State making such payments shall be reimbursed from funds herein appropriated. The amount of such reimbursement shall be determined by the Secretary of Labor on the basis of reports furnished to him by the States and such amount shall then be placed in the States unemployment trust fund account.

A person who, in connection with an occupational training program, has received a training allowance or whose unemployment compensation payments were reimbursed under the provisions of this Act or any other Federal Act shall not be entitled to training allowances under this Act for one year after the completion or other termination (for other than good cause) of the training with respect to which such allowance or payment was made.

No training allowance shall be paid to any person who is receiving training for an occupation which requires a training period of less than six days.

ON-THE-JOB TRAINING

The Secretary of Labor shall encourage, develop, and secure the adoption of programs for on-the-job training needed to equip persons selected for training with the appropriate skills. The Secretary shall, to the maximum extent possible, secure the adoption by the States and by private and public agencies, employers, trade associations, labor organizations and other industrial and community groups which he determines are qualified to conduct effective training programs under this title of such programs as he approves, and for this purpose he is authorized to enter into appropriate agreements with them.

In adopting or approving any training program under this part, and as a condition to the expenditure of funds for any such program, the Secretary shall make such arrangements as he deems necessary to insure adherence to appropriate training standards, including assurances—

(1) that the training content of the program is adequate, involves reasonable progression, and will result in the qualification of trainees for suitable employment;

(2) that the training period is reasonable and consistent with periods customarily required for comparable training;

(3) that adequate and safe facilities, and adequate personnel and records of attendance and progress are provided; and

(4) that the trainees are compensated by the employer at such rates, including periodic increases, as may be deemed reasonable under regulations hereinafter authorized, considering such factors as industry, geographical region, and trainee proficiency.

Where on-the-job training programs under this part require supplementary classroom instruction, appropriate arrangements for such instruction shall be agreed to by the Secretary of Health, Education, and Welfare and the Secretary of Labor.

NATIONAL ADVISORY COMMITTEE

The Secretary shall appoint a National Advisory Committee which shall consist of ten members and shall be composed of representatives of labor, management, agriculture, education, and training, and the public in general. From the members appointed to such

Committee the Secretary shall designate a Chairman. Such Committee, or any duly established subcommittee thereof, shall from time to time make recommendations to the Secretary relative to the carrying out of his duties under this Act. Such Committee shall hold not less than two meetings during each calendar year.

The National Advisory Committee shall encourage and assist in the organization on a plant, community, regional, or industry basis of labor-management-public committees and similar groups designed to further the purposes of this Act and may provide assistance to such groups, as well as existing groups organized for similar purposes, in effectuating such purposes.

DUTIES OF THE SECRETARY OF HEALTH, EDUCATION, AND WELFARE

The Secretary of Health, Education, and Welfare shall, pursuant to the provisions of this title, enter into agreements with States under which the appropriate State vocational education agencies will undertake to provide training needed to equip persons referred to the Secretary of Health, Education, and Welfare by the Secretary of Labor pursuant to section 202, for the occupations specified in the referrals. Such State agencies shall provide for such training through public education agencies or institutions or, if facilities or services of such agencies or institutions are not adequate for the purpose, through arrangements with private educational or training institutions. The State agency shall be paid 50 per centum of the cost to the State of carrying out the agreement, except that for the period ending June 30, 1964 the State agency shall be paid 100 per centum of the cost to the State of carrying out the agreement with respect to unemployed persons. Such agreements shall contain such other provisions as will promote effective administration (including provision (1) for reports on the attendance and performance of trainees, (2) for immediate certification to the Secretary of Labor by the responsible training agency with respect to each person referred for training who does not have a satisfactory attendance record or is not making satisfactory progress in such training absent good cause, and (3) for continuous supervision of the training programs conducted under the agreement to insure the quality and adequacy of the training provided), protect the United States against loss, and assure that the functions and duties to be carried out by such State agency are performed in such fashion as will carry out the purposes of this title. In the case of any State which does not enter into an agreement under this section, and in the case of any training which the State agency does not provide under such an agreement, the Secretary of Health, Education, and Welfare may provide the needed training by agreement or contract with public or private educational or training institutions.

APPROPRIATIONS AUTHORIZED

There are hereby authorized to be appropriated $2,000,000 for the fiscal year ending June 30, 1963, $3,000,000 for the fiscal year ending June 30, 1964, and a like amount for the fiscal year ending June 30, 1965, for the purpose of carrying out title I.

There are hereby authorized to be appropriated $97,000,000 for the fiscal year ending June 30, 1963, $161,000,000 for the fiscal year ending June 30, 1964, and a like amount for the fiscal year ending June 30, 1965, for the purpose of carrying out title II.

There are hereby authorized to be appropriated $1,000,000 for the fiscal year ending June 30, 1963, $1,000,000 for the fiscal year ending June 30, 1964, and a like amount for the fiscal year ending June 30, 1965, for the purpose of carrying out title III.

There are hereby authorized to be appropriated $5,000,000 for the fiscal year ending June 30, 1962, for planning and starting programs under this Act.